ST. JOSEPH'S UNIVERSITY

3 9353 00231 7079

WORK AND FAITH IN SOCIETY

A HANDBOOK FOR DIOCESES AND PARISHES

BR
115
.W67
W67

MAURICE L. MONETTE, OMI
EDITOR

SECRETARIAT
BISHOPS' COMMITTEE ON THE LAITY
NATIONAL CONFERENCE OF CATHOLIC BISHOPS

In its 1986 planning document, as approved by the general membership of the National Conference of Catholic Bishops in November 1985, the Secretariat of the Bishops' Committee on the Laity was authorized to publish a handbook that would deal with the interrelationship of work and faith. This publication, *Work and Faith in Society: A Handbook for Dioceses and Parishes*, continues the efforts begun at the 1983 lay convocation "Work and Faith in Society: Catholic Perspectives" and offers insight for those wishing to conduct similar consultations on the diocesan and parish levels. The text of this handbook has been approved by Dolores Leckey, Executive Director of the Bishops' Committee on the Laity Secretariat, and authorized for publication by the undersigned.

Monsignor Daniel F. Hoye
General Secretary
March 31, 1986

NCCB/USCC

ISBN 1-55586-988-2

Copyright © 1986
United States Catholic Conference, Inc.
1312 Massachusetts Avenue, N.W.
Washington, D.C. 20005-4105
All rights reserved.

CONTENTS

ACKNOWLEDGMENTS

The Laity Secretariat would like to thank the many people who contributed to this handbook. The speakers and participants in the "Work and Faith" conference, held at the University of Notre Dame, sparked the vision and confirmed the importance of this project. Bishop James Hoffman of Toledo, Ohio, former chairman of the NCCB Laity committee (1981-1984), and the bishops who served with him— Archbishop William D. Borders, Bishops Kenneth Untener, Howard Hubbard, William Houck, Daniel Hart, and William Weigand— encouraged open and exciting dialog, and their full participation in the conference was a critical element in its success. Mr. Neil Parent, adult education representative for the USCC Department of Education; Rev. Paul Rouse, director of liturgy for the Archdiocese of Boston; the staff of the Center for Pastoral and Social Ministry at Notre Dame— all generously contributed their expertise to the planning and facilitation of the conference. Finally, our thanks to Maurice L. Monette, OMI, who helped to shape this book, bringing it to fruition. To all, our deepest appreciation.

INTRODUCTION

Work and Faith in Society
Listening, Reflecting, and Acting

In 1980, the National Conference of Catholic Bishops approved a pastoral statement *Called and Gifted: The American Catholic Laity.* The last paragraph of that statement invited response on the calls to adulthood, holiness, ministry, and community.

To encourage dialog on the section dealing with Christian life in the world, the Committee on the Laity sponsored a conference at the University of Notre Dame, in October 1983, entitled "Work and Faith in Society: Catholic Perspectives." Its purpose was to listen to the experience of Catholic leaders in various occupations and to hear their reflections on the connection between work and faith. Questions that served as a background were (1) What is my life as a professional like? What does it have to do with my faith? (2) What kind of ministry challenges and supports me as a Christian? and (3) What are my expectations of the Church? How has the Church supported or failed me?

Approximately sixty men and women—self-identified Catholics, holding positions of responsibility and leadership in their occupations—were invited to the conference. Names surfaced in several ways: committee and staff brainstormed; we solicited suggestions from colleagues in other national offices; and each bishop in the NCCB was invited to submit names.

Participants came from twelve occupational groups: the arts; business; education; government/politics/diplomacy; human services and nonprofit organizations; labor; law and law enforcement; media; medicine and health; military and defense; science; and sports/entertainment. Our conference design included small groups for reflection, discussion, and recommendations; formal presentations; and open plenary discussions. There were times for prayer and worship and for informal conversation as well. All of these dynamics contributed to our learning.

The speakers, who were drawn from the participants, provided intellectual, spiritual, and emotional stimulus to explore the meaning of our lives as busy, responsible, professional lay Catholics. It is a selection of these talks, audio tapes, and written transcripts that comprise this handbook. The presentations, offered here, represent a richness of varied professional and personal experiences and a variety of perspectives.

Kenneth L. Woodward, senior writer for *Newsweek* and coauthor of *Grandparents/Grandchildren: The Vital Connection,* addressed the topic "Catholic Roots—Catholic Horizons?" In this the first presentation of the conference, Mr. Woodward talked about the whole of life: family, work, education.

The theme of "Professional Life: Vocation and Commitment" was addressed by two speakers, each drawing from personal experience. Dr. Sally Cunneen, an educator, focused on her personal continuing education from childhood to the present, with important insights about the ways and means for Christians to continue their inner growth intellectually, spiritually, and attitudinally. Mr. Ralph Graham Neas, executive director of the Leadership Conference on Civil Rights, spoke about coming to the realization that politics was and is his authentic vocation.

Dr. Doris Donnelly, theologian and author, had a slightly different task. She presented to the assembly the richness of the Catholic tradition—the laity's spiritual inheritance, as it were. She concentrated on prayer as a life-changing, life-giving encounter with the Lord. Her talk, "The Catholic Spiritual Tradition," invited everyone to a period of solitude and silence. Some walked the grounds of the university, some prayed in the chapel, others wrote in journals. This extended period of reflection prepared participants for the open forum that followed.

John A. Coleman, SJ, brought sociological expertise and vision to the deliberations. His talk, "The World Today and Tomorrow: Its Meaning for the Church," was an examination of the many social systems in which we all live and work. After laying out the future trends in these systems, Fr. Coleman addressed the question of what kind of ministry is needed, now and in the future, to enable busy lay people who are committed to secular vocations to be consciously Christian and "in the world."

Rev. James Bacik, a priest-theologian experienced in pastoral ministry and spiritual direction, was asked to observe closely the dynamics of the consultation and to note the major themes as they emerged in talks, in small groups, in social moments, in worship services—everywhere. In short, we asked him to be concentrated and alert to the marks of God in those two and one-half days when one significant segment of lay leadership was gathered together. His presentation reflected what had been voiced and felt throughout the days of the consultation; and it did so, brilliantly.

The overall task of the speakers was to ignite ideas and move the other participants to reflect on and share their experiences and values, as well as their doubts and needs, as lay Christians who wield secular power in some form. The speakers performed their task well. They animated the gathered leaders to make consciously the connection between Christian faith and the various fields of human work represented at the consultation.

Of the thirty-plus recommendations that came from eleven small groups, which met regularly during the consultation, many pointed to the need for similar consultations at the local level: in dioceses and in parishes. One group stated their recommendation in the following way:

> Recognizing that Christians engaged in common pursuits are often on opposing sides of complex issues, we recommend that the diocesan bishop provide mechanisms for these groups to convene to discuss how they see the issue from their shared faith and the teachings of the Church—not with a view to resolving the conflict but rather to reinforce their Christianity.

This handbook is an attempt to encourage dioceses, deaneries, and parishes "to step outside the church walls," to try something new, something that relates to the laity's role as the major Christian presence in the places of work and the places of culture. Think of this handbook as a resource for convening, listening to, and learning from lay people who are workers in industry, in education, in journalism, in medicine, in business—wherever Catholics (and other Christians) spend their working hours. The handbook's real value lies beyond the printed page, in the gatherings of men and women who are willing to grapple with the meaning of their working lives.

What is in the handbook?

Part I contains selected speeches from the "Work and Faith" consultation, with reflection and discussion questions at the end of each to prod your thinking. In this section, you will also find a synthesis of the participants' recommendations to the National Conference of Catholic Bishops and Bishop James R. Hoffman's report to the general assembly of the NCCB. Part I gives the reader a fairly comprehensive overview of the "Work and Faith" consultation and provides some stimulus for reflections on his or her experience of work.

Part II is a modest blueprint, indicating how others might design and conduct their own such consultation. There is a "how to" report, written by Patricia Davis, former staff assistant in the Laity Secretariat. This report, which first appeared as an article in the Winter 1984 issue of *Gifts*, describes in some detail how we went about putting together the consultation. Suggestions for dioceses and parishes as to how they might go about planning and conducting similar consultations and an example of what one deanery has already done are also found in this section.

Part III is a listing of various resources available through the United States Catholic Conference's Office of Publishing and Promotion Services, as well as those available elsewhere. These resources will be helpful to any group desiring to study this critical area of lay life.

In 1987, bishop representatives from all over the world will meet as a Synod on the topic of "The Vocation and Mission of the Laity in the Church and in the World." In preparation for this international event, Pope John Paul II has urged widespread consultation with the laity, regarding the various themes that characterize lay life. One of the most important aspects of the laity's life is surely their role in the secular sphere, where they are in science, culture, the arts, business, and so forth. Hopefully, this handbook will be one vehicle that will encourage diocesan and parish groups to focus on the laity's experience of being Christian in the world of work. It is an issue deserving of the Church's attention, not only because of the forthcoming Synod on the Laity, but because the mission of the Church and the laity's role in the world are woven together. It is an ongoing agenda for all of us.

Dolores Leckey
Executive Director
Secretariat
Bishops' Committee on the Laity

I.

REPORTING A NATIONAL
CONSULTATION

Work and Faith in Society
Selected Presentations

We have assembled here a selection of the presentations made during the conference. In order to stimulate the reader and provoke reflection, several questions follow each of the selected speeches.

Dr. Sally Cunneen and Mr. Ralph Graham Neas both addressed the topic of "Professional Life: Vocation and Commitment" from their different work perspectives, each bringing a personal view to the reconciliation of faith with the secular world of work.

As we planned the conference, we knew it was not enough to study only the stories of Catholics at work. If the conference were to be the dialog experience that the Laity Committee hoped it would be, then the other side of the Church's life—Catholics at prayer—had to be articulated. Dr. Doris Donnelly examined this other side when she spoke of "The Catholic Spiritual Tradition."

Because each one of us—as worker, spouse, friend, church person—lives in many systems that affect us in the present and into the future, we thought it important to study the laity's life in terms of social systems. Rev. John Coleman, SJ, was given this task and addressed the topic "The World Today and Tomorrow: Its Meaning for the Church."

The texts of these four presentations follow.

Continuing Education in the Church

Dr. Sally Cunneen

I would like to talk to you today about continuing education in the Church, and I would like to start in the *middle* where most good stories begin, because stories are critical to the kind of work I do.

I am a teacher of English composition and literature at my local community college in a suburban community about an hour north of Manhattan. I believe that the ability to say well what you want to say is a very potent force that is neglected today, and that ability should belong to everyone.

Having taught for fourteen years, I realize that it is only as my students—who are of very different ages (this is what we usually call continuing education or lifelong learning), adult students, people who work, people who have children, from very different economic, ethnic, and religious backgrounds—only as they come to see and affirm the actual circumstances of their lives, whether this is family, working, ethnic background, whatever, do they actually gain the ability to communicate and to deal with the circumstances of their lives.

Now, of course, an attitude like this keeps me in a running argument with the English department, or at least half of it, who believe that writing can be taught by rules. In my experience, the student who does not know who he or she is or where he or she has come from, in any reflective sense, cannot write the controlling thought which the English department tells you is the first thing you have to start your composition with—or at best it will not be *his* or *her* thought. Real writing, like thinking and feeling, is done by the whole person, so I have developed my own approach to help my students look freshly at their lives in order to develop their stories and learn to share them with others. I find that they are then much better able to hear the stories of other people without being threatened.

In interdisciplinary courses on central human concerns I call this thing "second sight," not only because the British call that a Gaelíc gift, but because it seems to me to sum up the natural magic involved when you can begin to understand and see the patterns of your own life. In courses like "Working People and Families," and "Human Freedom" we read imaginative stories in order to evoke the life stories. In every course I try to help students see that theories and stories themselves grew out of observation of people in living contexts, and that each one of us has a living laboratory from which to judge and assimilate whatever rings true.

I have learned a great deal from listening to students. Many tell stories of painful childhoods, experiences with drugs and alcohol, all the mistakes and sufferings imaginable, along with remarkable courage and humor. Such classes are often like United Nations sessions. In my last "Working People and Families" course one student told of his uncles' and grandparents' experiences of being in prison in the Austro-Hungarian empire. Next to him was a black woman from the locality, whose grandmother was a member of the Mohawk Indian tribe. The grandmother had been put out of the tribe at birth because she was deformed. She had been brought up by Quakers and when she was older she felt it her mission to go back and establish connections with the tribe. So she was able to pass down to her grandchildren a sense of identity that was much more powerful than those of the others in Nyack where she lived.

Such shared stories, I think, provide real information, pass it from old to young, and greatly expand the lives of those who thought the suburbs were boring. They confirm my own philosophy that life itself is the great educator, preceding our thinking about it, and that God's will for us can be read in the natural and the chance circumstances of our lives, if we reflect upon them and believe that our response to them is needed and wanted—and for that most of us need such a group to give support.

As I came to prepare for this unusual seminar, I realized that my present view of my teaching as vocation in community with the living Church has been the result of my own exceedingly long continuing education, one that I think is parallel to or, maybe even better, *part of* the continuing education of the American Catholic Church in my lifetime. By sharing some of the milestones on my journey of understanding how my faith could relate to the world, I hope to shed a little light on why we might be here for this conference and what difference it might make to the future of our work as Church.

In the world of my childhood I most certainly did not see the rootedness of ideas, imagination, and faith in the human story. Far from it. But in this I think I reflected the lack of understanding of my Church, as I experienced it, growing up in the East, coming to the end of its immigrant period, striving to establish itself as middle-class American, its theology and teaching somewhat defensive, unable to mediate the riches of its own tradition, still available, if one knew where to look. My Church's tendency to split Church and world, seeing neither quite clearly, was reinforced by my tendency to dwell on the imaginative.

My parents had introduced me to stories early, encouraging me to learn about the world through stories of other cultures. I pored over *National Geographic,* I loved myths and romances. Providence seemed very dull to me in comparison with King Arthur's Camelot or Robin Hood's Sherwood Forest. Under the disapproving eye of my sensible older sister who knew she wanted to be a nurse, I kept on taking fairy tales out of the library until I was thirteen, obviously needing, as Bruno Bettelheim has since informed us, much reassurance about the possibility of growing up at all in a world which seemed empty of the fantasy I craved.

No doubt my own sense of identity as a female was very complicated in the short term by my tendency to identify with King Arthur and Robin Hood instead of Maid Marion or the Lady of the Lake, who had exceedingly weak parts. In the long run it probably saved me from the "Cinderella Complex."

My parents taught me much more than love of reading, however. They were more secular than most of the parents in our parish. Both had gone to good colleges in Boston where they had encountered real prejudice. My father was told by a fraternity brother at M.I.T. that he was surprised not to see him wearing horns. His family had told him that all the Irish Catholics had horns. What my parents transmitted to me from such painful experiences reflected their own maturity. They took every occasion to recommend tolerance, interest, and support for every kind of person.

I remember my father telling me about the injustice done to Sacco and Vanzetti, a period he had lived, of course, and how he had spoken of the power of truth to convince even when it was expressed in poor grammar and without hope of personal success.

Above all, I also learned from my parents that women should do just about anything they wanted to. My father was remarkable, I learned much later, because he always pointed out to me women like Margaret Bourke White, Clare Boothe Luce, Babe Didrikson Zaharias, Helen Wills Moody. He was a big sports fan, and he made me feel that I could and should do similar things. Both my parents felt, of course, that I should do them well. Both of them worked. My father was a mechanical engineer; my mother had been a buyer for a department store. They felt that it was the joy of doing things to do them well, otherwise there was no point.

They offered me the world, but I was suspicious of it. I loved the Church. That appealed to my imagination. I identified with it, particularly through the liturgy, stations of the cross, the rosary, and the stories of the saints. Those stories from the Bible were pretty rationed when I was a child. They were considered potentially dangerous. Our education, however, tended to be rational and authoritarian. We did learn the useful habit of parsing sentences, but we did not learn to exercise our own curiosity or to trust our instincts.

I remember once when Sister St. John Joseph asked us why St. Joseph had been correctly guided by dreams but we were not. Staring at sixty dumbfounded faces she told us the answer: St. Joseph did not have the Church to guide him. Unfortunately, this guide did not help me see how as a Catholic I related to the actual city of Providence in which I was growing up. No one ever mentioned Roger Williams, for instance, no doubt considered a dangerous heretic for founding the city on principles of religious freedom.

My parents saw the connection. They saw connections with their own experience. They extended charity to realms of the intellect and spirit, but in St. Sebastian's—I actually *went* to that St. Sebastian's Kenneth Woodward heard about, you know—charity focused more on the physical needs of Catholics. It was not until I left the city that I realized that Catholics had actually been a *majority* in that city, *running* the place for a long, long time. The Irish, the Italians, and the French would just parcel out the offices. We had felt and thought as if we were a beleaguered minority in a hostile, yankee world.

So my *formal* Catholic education, though it nourished my belief in God, the practice of worship both public and private, and established certain ideals permanently, did not at all help me to see the connection between them and the world. Nor did it suggest anything I could do. The icon of St. Sebastian pierced with arrows did not help me in my search for a vocation. I felt torn between the values of my Church and my parents then, because I saw them as secular—wanting to be loyal to the best in both and not knowing exactly how. Now I know that nothing is a better motivator for an education than to be in such tension. It forces you to make a personal search for possible reconciliation.

Leaving home to go to college was my first milestone event. I went to the non-Catholic college my parents recommended, but I did not take the dangerous courses in philosophy or religion that my retreat director suggested I avoid. Being on guard, seeking, at the stage where Erikson tells us we are building identity, I found hope of unity in some rather unusual places. I found it in Gilson's lucid explanation, through an analysis of medieval philosophy, of how the individual seeking to fulfill self could in fact coincide with God's idea for that person. I found it in Bernanos' intense portraits of individuals, some female, living out their sanctity in struggle with an almost contemporary world. I discovered that personal intellectual work and struggle were always required of believers.

This intellectual discovery was reinforced by my encounter, just after graduation from college, with a French priest I met at a reception for foreign students in London. He was not used to American ways. He would not sit down anywhere with me. We had to keep walking. He thought it was not seemly for a priest to be seen with a woman. But as we walked all over London he gave me lessons that forced me to relate my life more thoughtfully to my life of worship.

"What do you take to Mass?" he would ask me. "My missal," I would reply. After several repetitions of this sort he had to tell me. "Yourself," he insisted, explaining that reflection on real shortcomings should precede the confiteor and that such thoughtful reflection would help me know God's will, the true desire of every prayer.

This same priest, still a close friend, hearing that I was soon to be married recommended a book to me called *No Priest Between Us.* This was a distinct change from the marriage manuals I had been offered in this country.

Helpful as all this advice was for the reconciliation of growth and intimacy and identity with the Church, it was still largely personal. But at the same time, in London I got to know the Young Christian Workers, chief among them, Pat Keegan, who was later to be one of the few laymen at the Second Vatican Council. He explained to me how his attitude toward God had changed during the war. He drew a small circle on a pad. Then he drew a few other circles. Then he drew lines between them. And he said, "Now, we all know that God made us and put us in one spot here," he said, pointing to the first circle. "That is our family and our home and that is where he expects us to start work. I have come a long way from the personal encounter with the Infinite I used to think of as a religious attitude." He pointed to the other circles. "That is where we do our religious education. Right here on the job with the people we meet in their homes, their shops, and the pubs we go to."

I would say the next thirty-odd years of marriage and putting out *Cross Currents* that came with the contract were variations on that theme—a theme that reconciled life, thought, work, and faith. From all over the world, Joe and I sought out thinkers and doers who were bridging the Church/world gap. We felt we needed to hear about these connections. It was our own education—getting leads from other Catholics with similar questions. The authors, no matter how brilliant, how famous, were invariably glad to share their stories with us—usually for nothing.

In the first issue, de Lubac set the tone by merging (this is 1950) the founding story of our faith in Genesis with the story of human development. "It is the seventh day now," de Lubac said. "God is resting and he is depending on us for the work that will continue the creation." Now that, of course, is in the Pope's encyclical.

Shortly after, in *Cross Currents*, Yves Congar broadened the definition of Church with his *fourfold* explanation, adding living human persons to the usual understanding of buildings, authority, tradition, and ideals. One of the important bridges that *Cross Currents* built for me was in relating faith to the need for politics. From Mounier to Archbishop Camara, the theme has been fruitful. In particular, I would cite a recent article by Leonardo Boff on the need for political saints which reflects the vital thinking of the Latin American Church on this issue today.

Another crucial bridge for me was that between psychology and religion. When I was young, you had to *choose* between psychology and the confessional. They were considered antagonistic. Articles by Father Ple, Oraison, Beirnaert, Buber and many others convinced me that Sister St. John Joseph was wrong. We still had to consult our dreams. But, more important than that, I came to see that the Church's sacraments pointed to the sacredness in the life passages which developmental psychologists outline. What the Church offered was the mission to go back and see the potential, and often the real holiness in birth, death, marriage, even in our common meals. The Eucharist, for example, is not only a symbolic meal of union; it is also a reminder that *all* meals are potentially already sacred: prepared by human beings out of natural living material, implying sacrifice whether of the onion or the lamb, all made by God but needing human participation and response to point in shared gratitude to the origin, as we suggest in the words of the Mass.

As a Catholic of the split Church/world era who dwelled too much in imagination, naturally it was the last wonder that I should discover the organic world itself. Having children, losing parents, set the life context. Reading Teilhard provided the mind-set, and being told by that brilliant, holy, funny man Raimundo Panikkar not to swat that fly—or, since he saw I was going to do it anyway, at least to think about what I was doing—brought the matter close to daily living. And finally, reading the elegant essays of Lewis Thomas (whom I was happy to see someone else had put on our reading list) confirmed the relationship between myself and the earth—ants, bees, snakes, shellfish—which I would never have dreamed possible in the early days when I thought nature not only boring and secular but, at best, protestant.

The simple and complex things of earth—food, trees, people—seemed more interesting *in themselves* as well as incarnations of God's artistry. Physical work which I, like Ken Woodward, used to avoid, became simply another and rather enjoyable mode of being. I came to appreciate the idea of the Benedictine Rule.

Before this however, in the mid-1960s, I felt compelled to struggle actively with my Church's notion of what adult women ought to do and be. It resulted in that book that Dolores Leckey mentioned to you that came out in 1968. Putting the questions with which I was wrestling into a questionnaire of 135 questions, supplemented by many interviews, I tapped a national sample of Catholics in 1965, including priests and laymen who answered with exceedingly interesting replies. But the response from women was extraordinary. Thousands answered. Hundreds wrote long, thoughtful questionnaires, thanking me, saying no one had *ever* asked them these questions before and that it forced them to think about central conflicts in their lives. In very personal stories, they stated their central concerns—the need for greater freedom of development within the church community and an overwhelming consensus that the Church exists to serve the world. And though this book did not effect the change in attitude I had hoped for from the official Church, the act of consultation itself affirmed my ability to act and think as Church on my own, feeling I was speaking for an *unofficial,* real constituency, though always in communion.

When I finished this book, I felt free to conceive of a vocation to teach, so I have come full circle in my quest for connections. My journey moved me from understanding the Church and world as split, separate, and antagonistic to understanding the Church as a way of relating to world, which points to God's presence in it, and asks for an individual response wherever we are. If "Outside the Church there is no salvation" was the motto of my childhood, the "Outside the world there is no salvation" which I heard last January from Edward Schillebeeckx marks the present. We have learned to see, often officially and in large parts of the teaching Church, that our mission is in and to the world.

I am not so sure, however, that we have understood quite as clearly that our identity, too, is of the world. Not only—as Karl Rahner put it—that we are a Church of sinners (that is more the world in the sense of flesh the biblical scholars clarified for us; that is in the Church as well as in the world, as Ken Woodward was telling you yesterday), but even more important is the notion that the Church is made up of people. I refer to world in the sense that it is open to sacred, that it is fallible when it speaks from too narrow a base. It *needs* to consult the faithful, as it is doing here. I learned this from that seminal article by Cardinal Newman that we printed quite some time ago called "Consulting the Faithful in Matters of Faith."

And it needs to share its lay connections, which are far deeper than any divisions of state in life, office, sex, or profession. Unlike that great American philosopher, Groucho Marx, who did not want to be a member of any club that would let him join, I am *happy* to be part of a Church that wants me as a member. But in the words of Albert Ple, in a very thoughtful assessment of his own continuing education in the Church through many painful periods of being silenced, "I am happy, yet unsatisfied, for I know that many lay people do not see themselves and their work, no matter how dedicated and excellent, as part of their being Church, and neither do their pastors."

I know that young people, those born after Catholics achieved the goal of entering mainstream American culture, have little sense that their faith demands intellectual and moral distinctions from them, particularly in questioning the dominant values of success in our country. They have not had the great blessing that I did of seeing it as a task for their lives. Yet my education suggests that we can only be

Church—the Church that we should be in these perilous times—if we can learn to demand much of all our members, then encourage their freedom of response and support them in their effort. If the spirit rises where it will, it is going to come up in some very surprising ways and people.

We as Church must learn to listen to some new stories, to support the tellers, to incorporate them in our living community. That is why I look forward to hearing more of your stories than I already have as we take part in this continuing education seminar of being Church.

Questions for Reflection

1. Just as Dr. Cunneen's life has been her forum for continuing education and reconciliation of the secular with the religious, so, too, has each one of us been formed as Church through a lifetime of development. What touchstones or turning points can you recall that brought you closer to a reconciliation of life, thought, work, and faith?

_____

_____

_____

_____

_____

2. Do you agree with Dr. Cunneen's philosophy that God's will for us can be read in the natural and chance circumstances of our lives? Why? How can you relate her philosophy to "second sight," as she defines the term?

_____

_____

_____

_____

_____

Politics as Vocation

Mr. Ralph Graham Neas

I cannot tell you what an honor it is to be here. I am still in shock, eight months after Dolores Leckey asked me to give this talk. I have had many opportunities to speak around the country, primarily with respect to civil rights issues and domestic policy issues, but never before have I had this type of opportunity. And I am not certain that I have ever learned so much so quickly. Hopefully I will be able, in a short amount of time, to share some important things with you. I want to commend Bishop Hoffman, Dolores Leckey, and scores of other people who put this symposium together. When I read the participants' biographies for the first time I was awed and, having met most of you in the last twenty-four hours, I am even more impressed.

This is a very special time for me. In addition to all the issues we are discussing, coming back here to address this conference at Notre Dame is also special. I am from the class of 1968, and as Ken Woodward described last night, it was a watershed year. I think if you listen to my story today and see the central themes and the importance of Notre Dame in my life, it will certainly corroborate some of the things Ken said with respect to that watershed time, as well as corroborate some of the things that I am doing now.

Within a couple of hours of arriving at Notre Dame (I came with my best friend from Notre Dame), I ran into my best friend from high school and his wife at the stadium. Several hours later I met my English professor from Marmion Military Academy who is now a rector at Saint Edward's Hall. So this has been a coming home in many, many different ways, certainly proving inaccurate some of what Thomas Wolfe has said.

But most important, it has been a rare opportunity for me to sit back and listen and to assess things. It has been a chance for me to assess my roles as a Catholic and as someone who is involved in politics, as well as an opportunity to hear from all of you. I learned a lot from listening to Dr. Cunneen and Ken Woodward—I must admit I was not expecting everything that I heard. I thought Ken's talk was extremely provocative as a good keynote speech should be. I believe I can incorporate some of the things Ken said into my remarks and, hopefully, add a few.

I would like to—at Dolores Leckey's request—explain why I am in politics and share with you some of the personal experiences that led me to politics, and, perhaps more importantly, those that have kept me in politics.

Dolores covered some of the more relevant parts of my life, mentioning that I am a graduate of Notre Dame. I am also a graduate of the University of Chicago Law School, which was a counterbalance in a positive way to the University of Notre Dame; I learned much there. I immediately went from Chicago to Washington, D.C. and joined the staff of Senator Edward Brooke. I was his chief legislative assistant for six years. When he was defeated in 1978, I joined the staff of Senator Dave Durenberger. After the Durenberger experience of two years, I figured eight years were enough as a chief legislative assistant on Capitol Hill, which is primarily an alter-ego role, as exciting and fulfilling as it was, and I went with the Leadership Conference on Civil Rights. As Dolores pointed out, it is a coalition of 165 national organizations—women's groups, black groups, Hispanic groups, senior citizen groups, disability groups, labor groups, and many, many others. It is my job—sometimes an impossible job—to try to reach a consensus among those groups with respect to what priorities they want to pursue in a particular congress, in a particular administration.

A. Philip Randolph, Roy Wilkins, and Arnold Aronson formed the Leadership Conference back in 1950. The conference spearheaded the effort to enact the 1957 bill on civil rights, the 1964 Civil Rights Act, the Voting Rights Act, and the Fair Housing Act. We coordinated the national campaign on the voting rights extension in 1981 and 1982. We are currently involved in many struggles, such as the Fair Housing Bill. I have to go back to Washington early this afternoon, unfortunately, because we are marking up the extension of the Civil Rights Commission tomorrow morning, and Senator Biden has asked to see me tonight. We are trying to preserve a bipartisan, independent commission following the president's attempt to fire several members of the commission back in May of 1983. We are also working on the

Equal Rights Amendment. We are working on the Women's Economic Equity Act—that was the last bill that I drafted while still with Senator David Durenberger—which eliminates discrimination with respect to women in the areas of insurance, Social Security, pensions, taxes, and child support.

We are also fighting many rear-guard actions. I will try not to be political in a partisan way today, but there are assaults, obviously, on many of the issues that many of you, and certainly those in the civil rights community, care about. This is a time of some progress, but, frankly, we have to spend a lot of our time just protecting what was accomplished during the 1960s and the 1970s. Many of us have a fear that this could be, if we are not careful, an era of a second post-Reconstruction where many of the gains of a generation are wiped away in a very short time.

How did I get to Washington, D.C., and what led me to a career in politics? I believe two things were primarily involved: my Catholic upbringing and education, as provided by the Church and by my family, and growing up in the 1950s and 1960s. Many of my earliest recollections regarding the Church and my family include themes which have been constant and sometimes dominant throughout my life. I think the development of a social conscience was in large part due to the teachings of the Church which state that God did not put us here on earth only for ourselves or only for our families. We are supposed to reach out and strive to make this place a better place for everyone in the world and hopefully, by doing so, making ourselves better. The second commandment, "Thou shalt love thy neighbor . . ." is something we all learn when we are six or seven years old. But that was my first experience with the dignity of the individual, and how we are supposed to treat one another.

I learned equality before God long before I learned equality before the law. There are the passages from St. Luke that command us to attend to the poor, the sick, and the needy. I have seen that same language incorporated into the bishops' ministry in the world as set forth in *Called and Gifted,* which was given to us by Dolores Leckey and Bishop Hoffman. That publication addresses issues of peace and justice, especially as they influence the poor, the oppressed, and minorities. The Second Vatican Council came up with a statement that I will always remember: All discrimination should be eradicated because it is contrary to God's law.

The 1960s—my time here at Notre Dame—were tumultuous. We had graphic evidence on TV and radio and in the newspapers of serious and pervasive discrimination in our country. You could watch the evening news and see the results of the Birmingham church bombings. You could see the march to Selma. You could see "Bull" Connors beating up blacks before your very eyes. You could see state troopers using electric cattle prods on human beings. You could see Martin Luther King and the Kennedys and witness their leadership. We discovered that discrimination was a serious problem. It was much more flagrant at that time, much more obvious. But, as most of us know, it is still with us. It is simply more subtle and sophisticated. Those events, however, were my first confrontation with the pervasiveness of discrimination—how fate or government action or private action can deprive individuals of equality of opportunity, deprive individuals of the right to achieve their fullest potential. I learned that it was not only a Christian duty to try to address these wrongs, but, it was made clear to me, if we do not act, that lack of action only guarantees that these problems will some day engulf us all. We have got to do something about them.

How do we take action against these problems? In the 1960s I was not sure. At Marmion Military Academy a number of the fathers tried to talk me into joining the priesthood. I told them that I did not think I had the discipline needed, and I just did not feel it was the calling for me, although I was tempted many times because I consider the priesthood, above many things, to be public service, and I did want to get into public service. That desire led me to politics which, in turn, led me to Notre Dame and to one of my first role models, Father Theodore Hesburgh, who seemed to combine the best of Church and state. It brought me to the University of Chicago Law School, and, frankly, it was not to become a lawyer to practice law. Rather, it was to become a lawyer to put the tools of the law to service on behalf of people in government or in some type of public service.

Politics was for me a way to address the problems I saw, a way to get things done. Politics seemed to be the art of the possible. Sometimes it is strange to hear me say some of these things, having been in Washington for a decade and arriving right in the middle of the Vietnam War, right at the start of Watergate, right in the middle of all the corruption. And I know that the stock of politicians has plummeted—many times for good cause. However, I believe the general impression is most unfortunate and destructive. For I believe, in the words of Senator Phil Hart from Michigan who died a couple of years ago, that politics is a high vocation. A politician, to use an old expression, is the lay priest of society. The corporal works of mercy are part of the business of how the government runs. I regard it as an opportunity to make a humane life for everyone. For me, politics is one of the best means of implementing what I have learned from the Catholic Church and from my family. And through politics, in that nitty-gritty real world, you *can* affect millions of people in a positive way. You *can* provide that equality of opportunity and help those people achieve their fullest potential. Jimmy Carter once said, "Life is unfair." Jimmy Carter, in this case, was right. But I believe government can be a positive force and can help make life fairer.

Why am I still there? What has happened over the past decade in light of some of the things that I mentioned to keep me there? Certainly one of the reasons is the type of individual that I worked for—Senators Ed Brooke and Dave Durenberger are two exemplary politicians, two people who incorporate everything that I have talked about. They were good role models, as were Hubert Humphrey, Philip Hart, and others.

But about four years ago something happened to me that, perhaps more than anything else, is responsible for my staying in Washington and for my work in the Leadership Conference. On Valentine's Day of 1979, I was stricken with Guillain-Barré Syndrome, a disease that paralyzes the nerves and, consequently, the muscles. Over a period of weeks I became totally paralyzed. I could not talk; machines breathed for me; machines fed me and took care of every other vital function. I lost fifty pounds and went from about 160 to 110 pounds. I was in terrible pain and was given general absolution. I fought for life on the critical list for about three and one-half months. I regard that experience as one of the central learning lessons of my life and I would like to share a few of the lessons that I learned from that experience.

When I went into the hospital, one of the first persons I met, outside of the nurses in Intensive Care, was a woman named Sister Margaret Francis Shilling, who was to become my most unusual role model. Sister Margaret was a seventy-three-year-old nun at that time. On her twenty-fifth anniversary as a nun, she had contracted Guillain-Barré

Syndrome; on her fiftieth anniversary as a nun, she met me. Needless to say, I looked around the hospital and figured that it might be the place for me if I had to go through something like that.

The next day I met two of my doctors. One of them was Pat Barrett. He was the chief doctor at the hospital and a graduate of Notre Dame. A couple of weeks later I met my surgeon, another Notre Dame graduate. When they came to me and asked whether I wanted to go to the Mayo Clinic where the care might be more sophisticated, I said, "No, I think I will stay right here. I think this might be the place for me for the next couple of months." And it *was* the place.

Sister Margaret was my spiritual advisor. She obviously could share with me what I would experience with Guillain-Barré, and because I could not talk for three months, she was the person who could most effectively communicate with me. She was the person who saved my life, helped me spiritually, and really renewed much of my faith. She underscored my faith and helped me learn several basic lessons which I would like to share with you right now—lessons that are particularly applicable to a (at that time) thirty-two-year-old bachelor in Washington, D.C., but lessons that will be helpful also to others—because at age thirty-two I went through an experience that most people will have only at the end of their lives.

The first lesson was vulnerability. I was a thirty-two-year-old so-called Washington hot-shot on the fast track on Capitol Hill. I was chief legislative assistant to one of the best, most famous, and most effective senators. I was riding the crest of the wave of success and, of course, when one is riding the crest of success, you do not pause too often to think about what you are doing, how you got there, or what you want to do with it. You are having fun. You think that you are doing good things, but you never pause. You never think it through. You certainly do not take into consideration acts of God or the fact that you are as vulnerable as anyone, no matter how hard you work. I always believed that as long as I put in the Neas effort and worked hard, no matter what I wanted to achieve, I would achieve it. Well, that is not a bad threshold philosophy, but it is certainly not enough. I found that out very, very rapidly. I was very vulnerable.

I was also to become very dependent. As that thirty-two-year-old bachelor in Washington, D.C., without any marital or parental responsibilities, I was Mr. Independence. I could do anything I wanted whenever I wanted to do it. I did not need other people. Oh, I needed friends; I had terrific friends. I had a terrific job, but basically it was Ralph Neas by himself taking on the world, having fun, and accomplishing some good things, hopefully, but not recognizing the interdependence that makes this world go around.

Within a matter of days—weeks—I was totally dependent on machines. I was also dependent on friends. I received a couple of thousand letters from people while I was in the hospital that were read to me by Sister Margaret. They buoyed my spirits. They kept me going during the pain, during the twenty-four-hour days, maybe about twenty-two hours of which I had to stay awake. Every twenty minutes they would rotate me because of the tremendous weight loss, so I would not get infections. Every twenty to thirty minutes they would have to suction my lungs out because of the pneumonia problems. Those letters, those friends, came through for me time and again. Sister Margaret would come at least a couple of times a day and hold my hand and talk to me, talk about anything, make jokes, talk about my strange friends back in Washington, D.C., and about what a plastic place it seemed to be. It just did not seem real, which has more than a grain of truth.

I got a letter from Digger Phelps, another friend who is here today. That letter came right after Notre Dame's loss to Michigan State in the NCAA tournament back in 1979. It meant a lot. Digger was probably in a state of some depression, certainly cooling down after a bad season. Of course what I did not tell Digger when I came out of the hospital was that the three losses at the end of the season—I think they were to Michigan, De Paul and Michigan State—followed the course of my disease. The first loss was the day before I came down with Guillain-Barré, the second loss was the day before I had my tracheotomy because of the respiratory failure, the third and final loss was the day before I had my general absolution. All I could think of was, "Digger, thank God the season's over."

Another Notre Damer came through for me. He is a friend of Digger and a friend of mine. In fact, Nordy introduced me to Digger. He is Nordy Hoffman, a Football Hall of Famer, a Knute Rockne protégé, and a former sergeant-at-arms of the United States Senate. Nordy Hoffman is one heck of a person, and during March of 1979 he was in charge of Universal Notre Dame Night. I had one particularly difficult period of about two weeks where it was a day-to-day struggle to survive, whether I was going to live or not. The key night was March 22, 1979. I developed blood clots in my lungs, and I was in very bad shape. By the end of the night I had made peace with God, said goodbye to my parents and my friends, and thought I had done everything possible to stay alive. But, I just did not have any strength left. Little did I know—and I would not find out for five more months—but that night there was a dinner I was supposed to attend, a dinner at which Digger has spoken many times—Universal Notre Dame Night. And, at that dinner, at the very same time I was fighting desperately to live, Nordy Hoffman was leading the Notre Dame crowd of 500 in a prayer for me. You can well imagine my reaction many months later when I realized that in those moments of my greatest need, there were so many Notre Damers praying for my recovery. No wonder I believe so fervently in the spirit of Notre Dame!

In early May 1979, I began the reversal phase of my bout with Guillain-Barré. Every day it became clearer that I would live and that most likely I would recover fully from the state of paralysis. Because of my progress, I knew that I would soon be having a heart-to-heart talk with my mother about my future plans.

Just before my mother came for a visit, Sister came and we talked. It was the first week off my respirator so I could actually talk. They would put a little cork in my trachea and I would take a deep breath and I could talk for a while. I told Sister Margaret that my mother was going to come in and she was going to give her "mother's speech" which would be, "It is time to get out of politics; it is time to marry; it is time to settle down; it is time to practice law. Haven't you learned your lesson now?" So I said, "Sister I want you to stick up for me; you know me, perhaps as well as anybody else knows me. You have seen me, and you know what I would like to do with my life. I need a back-up here. I need a support system. Would you stay for this meeting?" She said, "Of course, I will."

So I went into the reasons with my mother, as a tear or two came down her cheeks, of why I wanted to go back to Washington and not Chicago, why I did not want to return to my law firm but wanted to go back and continue my work with Dave Durenberger. She took it fairly well. It was pretty tough for her to combat both me and Sister Margaret Francis under those circumstances. That decision led me back to Washington and back to Dave Durenberger and, frankly, prepared the way for my acceptance of the job with the Leadership Conference on Civil Rights.

The job with the Leadership Conference was mentioned to me while I was still with Dave Durenberger. I thought it would be a good job but I did want to take some time off. Needless to say, after the year with Guillain-Barré I thought that I should have a sabbatical and think through a few things, and, most importantly, get my strength back. It takes about a year for your muscles to return to their vitality and to get everything moving again. It is a reversible syndrome if you live through it and have a little bit of luck. So I took that sabbatical and, in the meantime, I found that there had been some opposition developing to my candidacy—my being a white male Republican Catholic. I think it was somewhat understandable that Vernon Jordan, Ben Hooks, and others might have felt there was perhaps someone else better suited for the job. Of course it would have been exceptionally ironic, but I would have accepted it, if I had become a victim of affirmative action. However, that was the way it was for several months.

It was not a job for which I campaigned. I was truly honored when Clarence Mitchell came to me. It was a job that I devoutly wished for while I was an aide to Senator Brooke, but I thought that it was something they would have to spend time thinking through. They did go after Eleanor Holmes Norton, Ron Brown, and many other friends of mine, but for various reasons none of them could take the job. So it was offered to me in March 1981. And surprisingly—perhaps not so surprisingly—Ed Brooke, Dave Durenberger, and many others said, "You spent ten years doing this job; it is time to go on to other things. Your mother really is right; you really should try to establish some financial security; you should have a family; you should be doing other things."

I told them that I had learned a lot of things, and those lessons had been reinforced by my experience in the hospital. I had been given these experiences for some reason. I had been given certain gifts for some reason, and the Leadership Conference job was a once-in-a-lifetime opportunity to put these gifts to use. My work with Ed Brooke had prepared me professionally for this type of occasion, and my experience in the hospital had certainly prepared me psychologically.

So I did take the job and I have had a fascinating two and one-half years. It is enjoyable work, but it really is hard work, Ken, and I know that you know that. I know that everyone here realizes when you get into work, when you do put in those twelve-, fifteen-, or eighteen-hour days, the adrenalin is pumping and you love it. You think that this important self-sacrifice is, in many ways, self-fulfillment. And that is the nature of my job.

In conclusion, I think that the next ten or twenty years are going to be extraordinarily important for so many reasons. Those seemingly insurmountable problems of peace and justice will dominate the next decade or two: whether we are going to survive as a world; whether we are going to address those economic opportunity issues, not just here in the United States, but—as Digger and I were talking about last night—in the Third World and, indeed, around the entire world; whether we are going to address the debt problem; and the threat of a nuclear holocaust. We have got to start addressing and resolving these problems.

We know that an individual can make a difference, and we know individuals working together can make a big difference. When we work in partnership, as we are here today, that is when we start effecting some change.

Yesterday and today, as I have said, have been immensely valuable to me. Ken Woodward's presentation and Sally Cunneen's presentation were extraordinary and very instructive for me. In some ways they were not *enough* for me because they left certain things out, understandably so. And frankly, my presentation is not enough for me by any means because I am still struggling with a lot of things. I am still searching, and this conference has been most helpful in that search. I came back to Notre Dame, and, as usual, my role models are here. Seeing Father Ted Hesburgh last night and hearing more history about Notre Dame than I had ever heard in twenty years as a Notre Damer, meeting with Father Gremillion afterwards in the Institute of Pastoral and Social Ministry, that to me is what it is all about. That is what Notre Dame meant to me while I was here—preparing the Catholic laity for the world outside, preparing them to get into the nitty-gritty of the real world and, with their Catholic values, to do something about the real world.

If you take us all together this is a community of conscience. There are so many different vocations here, and I have obviously been addressing only one. But in the hospital, in my work in Washington, and certainly here you recognize the interdependence of these vocations. We must continue to cooperate, we must—in the words of my group last night—continue to reinforce one another, learn from one another, and we must do our jobs together. I thank you very much.

Questions for Reflection

1. Mr. Neas uses the expression, "a politician is the lay priest of society." What do you think is meant by this? Can you think of some specific scripture passages that might incorporate politics and biblical teaching?

_____

_____

_____

_____

_____

2. The Second Vatican Council stated that all discrimination should be eradicated because it is contrary to God's law. What are some of the ways in which people are being discriminated against in today's society? What role can the Church play in correcting these abuses and effecting change? How can you, as a Christian, help to address these problem areas in your everyday life?

_____

_____

_____

_____

_____

The Catholic Spiritual Tradition

Dr. Doris Donnelly

The story is told of a man who visited a bird store for the very first time. He saw birds on perches and birds in cages and birds flying about the store. Puzzled by one thing he approached the owner of the store. "I noticed," he said, "that all of these birds have a tag around their feet and a number on those tags. What does it all mean?" "Simple," said the owner of the store. "That is the price of the bird. You see, these birds are for sale. We have birds in all price ranges. We have birds starting at $5, and they go all the way up to $100, but for $100 you get a very special bird. You get a bird that can converse with you just as you and I are conversing right now." "Fine," said the visitor to the bird store. "Wrap up one of those $100 birds and I will take it home." And he did.

The next day the owner of the bird returned to the bird store. "My bird is not talking," he said. "I am not surprised," said the owner of the bird store. "You left here in such a hurry yesterday I forgot to tell you that you must bring home a bell for your bird. After all, don't you need a bell to get you going in the morning? Don't you need an alarm clock or a clock radio or the TV to get you going?" It made sense to the owner of the bird, so he said, "Fine. Wrap me up a bell and I will take it home." And he did.

On the third day the owner of the bird returned to the bird store. "My bird is still not talking. Do you think I should be worried about this?" asked the owner of the bird. "No, I would not worry about it," said the owner of the store. "But I was thinking about you and your bird last night and I think what your bird needs is a mirror. Your bird is dislocated. Your bird does not know where he is. But if he has a mirror to look himself in the face, then that will help him, and he will start talking in no time." "Fine," said the owner of the bird. "Wrap me up a mirror and I will take it home." And he did.

The following day the owner of the bird returned to the bird store.

"My bird is still not talking," he said somewhat anxiously. "You know, when your bird was in this store," said the owner of the store, "your bird traveled all around this store. He traveled from one end to the other and now your bird is confined to a tiny cage. I think your bird needs exercise. I promise you if you bring home a ladder, that is what your bird needs to start him talking." "Fine," said the owner of the bird. "Wrap up a ladder and I will bring it home." And he did.

On the fifth day, the owner of the bird returned to the bird store. "My bird is still not talking!" he said. "I have tried all these things! I have tried the bell, I have tried the mirror, I have tried the ladder; and my bird is still not talking! A hundred bucks for a bird, and he is still not talking!" he said. "I am not surprised," said the owner of the store. "Look at you, you are a nervous wreck. You are communicating your anxiety and your tension to this poor little bird. No wonder this bird is not talking. You know what your bird needs? He needs a little vacation. I would recommend that you buy your bird a swing. He needs to learn to relax." "It sounds incredible to me," said the owner of the bird, "but I will spring for a swing," he said. "And I will bring it home, and I sure hope this one works." And he did.

And on the sixth day, the owner of the bird arrived at the store. "My bird is dead," he said. "Oh, how awful," said the owner of the store. "But, tell me, did he talk before he died?" "He talked, all right!" said the owner of the bird. "I want to tell you exactly what happened. He woke up this morning and hopped over to his little bell and pecked it with his little beak, and it was a perfect F-sharp. And then he jogged over to his little mirror, and I tell you, if birds could smile, that bird smiled. And then he went over to his ladder. And he went up that ladder and down that ladder ten times. And then he hopped over to his little swing. And I saw him swing back and forth and back and forth. And right before he keeled over, I heard him say, quite distinctly, 'Didn't they have any bird seed?' "

I have come today to talk about bird seed. I have come today to talk about prayer, the heart of the Christian experience.

It may be comforting for you to know that in the glowing post-Camelot days of the Second Vatican Council there were many people determined not to forget the bird seed. The spirit of Vatican II catapulted the laity from second-class citizenship, where they were traditionally expected to pay, pray, and obey, to first-class status. The laity moved from the area of negative definition—what they did not have and could not do—into positions as living tissue and membrane in the Body of Christ. And there were many people who yielded attractive accessories for the central and centering experience of prayer. A call to renewal was sounded and the laity were ready.

You know there was no way to forecast, while Catholics were jettisoning so many traditional religious practices, that there would be a zealousness about contemplation, asceticism, retreats (even lengthy retreats), spiritual direction, simplicity of life style, meditation, and other assorted spiritual exercises. Let it be said, simply, that the ground was cosmically fertile, and that the laity responded with a sincerity, seriousness, and ardor that surprised many, including many of the laity themselves. The curious update on all of this, twenty years after the Second Vatican Council, is that while there is a sense, in some circles, that the laity had been demoted to the back of the bus and that the brakes had been applied to the influence and participation of the laity, there is not now, nor has there ever been, a way to apply the brakes to the movement of the Holy Spirit. It will be the guidance of that Holy Spirit that will carry us all—laity, clergy, hierarchy, alike—to fulfilling our mission in the Church.

And that is the subject of my time with you this afternoon—a closer feel, perhaps, of the gust of this Spirit as it breathes through three things: our identity, our work, and our growth. I want to take these three themes and view them as the person who prays knows them, and then touch upon how they might be experienced in daily church life by the layman or laywoman. The first theme is identity; the second is work; the third is growth; the parallel tracks deal with what the prayer life of the Christian tells us about these themes and how they might be reinforced in the daily life of the Church.

Identity. Christian identity is best—more than that, it is *only*—discovered in prayer. In prayer, as in nowhere else—although I am helped in prayer if I have human experiences of acceptance and openness that I can count on and relate to—am I able to risk being stripped bare, unmasked, and stand before God who loves me so convincingly and so totally that the event is not masochistic and cruel, but freeing and healing. It is there, when I unmask myself and stand before God, that I catch a glimmer—just a little insight—of the real me, surrender what is phony, and yield to someone who knows me better than I know myself. The grace that enables this to happen—and it is a grace you will identify with as soon as you hear it—is the gift of transparency.

Transparency is the gift of not standing in the way and of letting God's life and being shine through us and what we do. Transparency means letting the ego get out of the way, dropping all masks, disguises, pretenses, conquering what we call the "false-self," and standing as a naked and solitary individual before God. It is a daring and uncomfortable place to be, but one that we all know is the absolute prerequisite for honest, religious living.

I have a love-hate reaction to this thing happening; I suspect you do, too. Let us be frank about it. We sense the more we can be. We sense a disillusionment with things as they are, even an excitement over the self-discovery that comes in prayer. But there is, at the same time, a fluttering in the stomach that accompanies all adventures with the unknown. A fear that, in the stripping away, something vital that I cannot live without will be taken or the chance that God will do something with me that I had not intended. Some, however, live transparently as a matter of course. Francis of Assisi was such a person; others claim that the gift was part-and-parcel of Dorothy Day's life; and some suggest Thomas More was joyful and transparent all the way to the scaffold. I am inclined to believe all of those stories.

Thomas More's biographer suggests that the spirit of Christ invaded his very being. This is how it happens. Therefore, one can see straight through the person to Christ, no one stands in the way. Like Francis of Assisi, Thomas More made no bones about the fact that his personality, character, psychological development depended entirely on the imitation of Christ. His model was Jesus who articulated the classic statement on transparency when he said that the one who saw him saw God (Jn 12:45). Transparency was such a vital and intrinsic part of Thomas More's life—perhaps of Dorothy Day's life, and some of your lives as well—that he could have also said the same thing. It was through this grace of transparency that More and others discovered themselves and found their identity interwoven with Christ's. "Now it is not I who live, but Christ in me."

I want to move briefly over to the blackboard and illustrate my point, because I was called on to be a resource person in this area of spirituality. I am going to show you how this gift of transparency works in any of the major Western spiritual classics that you may have read. I think it works perfectly with John of the Cross and Teresa of Avila, but let me illustrate it for you. If you have questions about this later and you would like me to relate it to you again, I will be happy to do so.

We are talking about the gift of transparency. That is how I discover my identity. These are repeated figures. It says figure one here. This is the movement of any spiritual journey. When you have classics and spirituality where people are writing about that spiritual journey, this is what it looks like when it comes to identity. The dots in each circle represent an individual. This blank space here, around the dot, is Christ's life in the individual.

Figure one represents us at the beginning of the spiritual journey with what we call the "false-self" or the ego—very big, very dominant, and most important of all, very center stage. I am my existence. I am in the middle of everything. Big ego. Big "false-self." I have to be heard. I have to be running things. In the spiritual journey, very quickly, we have a thing called—it sounds terribly psychological and it is, but it is transposed also into spiritual terms—ego-reduction. Notice the size of the ego in figure one; it is massive and centered. But it has been reduced in figure two. That is all we can say. It has been reduced significantly, but it is still at center stage. The ego has been reduced by the activity of grace and prayer and by opening ourselves in service to our brothers and sisters. A very significant thing has happened.

In figure three, we not only have an ego reduced, we have an ego decentered. Now the center of that person's life is Jesus Christ. In this figure the ego is decentered and it is going to die. That "false-self," that "not-real-me" is going to die, and Christ is going to live in the person. This is going to be the beginning of the transparency. Here you have Christ's life in the individual's life.

Something else very important happens when the ego, when the "false-self," dies: The real self is born. This is a theory that I have devised and it works; but, in the confines of a conference like this where I have to discuss it so briefly, you may have questions about it later. Christ lives in me, but also something is born in me—my real self.

Then I go through a period of struggle with my real self. I want my real self to be not I who lives separately, but Christ in me, and so I move closer and closer to union with God, with Jesus Christ. I get a taste of this union and then I withdraw. This is a period of tasting it and then withdrawing, tasting it and then withdrawing. This is what enables me—this stage and this stage—to sense in some of my role models someone who has connected with the Lord. I know it because

I have tasted it. I know what I would have to yield to be there myself. That spiritual journey ends with the real transparent person. This is the symbolic representation of saying, "Not I live, but Christ in me." It is a long struggle of ego-reduction, ego-decentering, ego-death, which everyone talks about, so that Christ can live more fully in me; I can get a taste of it, pull away, and then end up as the real transparent person.

When we look at the transparent person, we look through the person and we say that we see Christ. She is working with the hands of Christ. He is ministering with the hands of Christ—the mind of Christ. We are putting on the mind of Christ. That is what it looks like when we look at that person, but that is only half the story. That explains how we look at the person, but now we have to get into the person looking out at the world. In other words, let us get in the shoes of a Thomas More or a Francis of Assisi or a Dorothy Day. We have to look at the other side of things—at what it looks like from their place, and, in so doing, we learn three important things about transparency. Incidentally, John Donne who is a professor here at the University of Notre Dame has followed exactly this journey in all of his books, and the latest metaphor he has really latched onto in his book *The Church of the Poor Devil* is this metaphor of transparency. One could take that book and just superimpose it on what I am saying: By putting ourselves in the place of the person we are looking at, this person looking out on the world, we learn three things about transparency.

First, to live transparently is to live freely. Transparent persons—think of Dorothy Day, think of the people in your own lives, think of Francis of Assisi—are free, unencumbered by things, especially those things that wind up possessing us more than we possess them: the car we drive, the neighborhood we live in, the microwave, the Betamax. *Things* always hinder the see-through quality of transparency. That is why transparent persons always feel a distance from those conversations that are about accumulations of what I own, what I did, and whom I know. This seeing, which sees *through* those things, makes it hard to enter into dialog with people who live by things. People who are transparent struggle with life style.

Second, to live transparently is to see the world as God sees it and to love it with God's love. This morning Dr. Cunneen mentioned Lewis Thomas and the widening of the world of nature. People who are transparent do not love selectively; they do not decide whom they are going to love. They do not cautiously dole out their love to people, but rather they experience a grand sweep of love for all, since the mighty and the lowly are both precious in the eyes of God.

And third, to live transparently reinforces the theological truth that, having been baptized, we all participate in the fullness of Christian life.

Last night Ted Hesburgh mentioned the dissertation he wrote on the priesthood of all believers and how he struggled to get it assigned to him. The curious thing about that is, in preparing for this confer-ence, I did some research on the priesthood of all believers; there has not been much progress since he wrote his dissertation. It is a very curious thing because in prayer, you see, there is no discrimination. People who pray do not feel the discrimination of the Holy Spirit saying, "I am sorry. You cannot go further; you are simply laity. I am sorry, you are a woman and you cannot progress to stage number four or five or figure number six. Because you are this you cannot. . . ." People in prayer do not have any of those experiences at all. However, very frequently in the daily life of the Church they do.

And it is also curious to me that, not only in the Roman Catholic Church, but also in Protestant denominations, the priesthood of all believers never caught on. I suspect the reason why is the same across denominational lines. Human nature being what it is, the priesthood of all believers and its implications of an egalitarian approach to ministry remain rather threatening to many ordained clergy of whatever denomination. Instead of looking upon the common baptism as a commitment to, and joint effort for, the same Lord, it is sometimes warily regarded as usurping powers that belong to a select few.

In a recent issue—it is a couple of years old now, but relatively recent—of *America* magazine, John Coleman who will be addressing us tomorrow raises this issue of the priesthood of all believers and talks about the future of ministry. But it is less his article and more the responses to it that interest me. Three of those responses were pub-lished. Two were written by permanent deacons who expressed surprise that Father Coleman was not aware that there was no need for a different ministry of the future that would involve laity. They felt that deacons were the answer—the only answer. These men gently scolded Father Coleman for opening a can of worms better left sealed. The last letter from a Jesuit priest painfully suggested that Father Coleman was guilty of breaking ranks and not adequately pedestaling the ordained priesthood.

I do not think I have overstated the case; nor have I exaggerated the truth that a high doctrine of the laity seems to strengthen rather than diminish a high doctrine of the ministry of ordained ministers and clergy, for it is simply so.

This is a good time for me to remind you of something that you are already aware of after participating in almost twenty-four hours of this symposium. We are in the presence of bishops who are amazingly open to our agendas, who have come as listeners to hear what we have to say. I think part of our responsibility—and I will surely bring this up in group two of which I am a member—is to encourage the bishops and the clergy who are listening to the laity. If what I hear is true regarding the goings-on at the Vatican at the present time, we are in for a whiff of severe conservatism overtaking the Church. And I would hate to see any criticism unfairly leveled at people who are supporting the laity now, for it is all the ammunition Rome will need to put a lid on the bottle that is holding the fresh air of the Second Vatican Council and the laity. I am not sure if that metaphor is appropriate, but you know what I mean.

Identity. We get it in prayer; we get it through transparency, looking at the person who is transparent and looking out. Let us talk a little bit about the theme of work. Actually, we want to talk about service, but in the words of this consultation we want to talk about work.

From the point of view of spirituality, the call to prayer and to life in the Spirit has a hitch to it. Anyone who prays knows of the foolish things that the love of God has us do. There is an outreach. Persons who pray quickly recognize that prayer is not, in the words of Evelyn Underhill, "a divine duet nor is it a blessed coma." The outreach from prayer is direct, immediate, painful, and real. The fact that a rigorous, committed prayer life leads to solidarity with our brothers and sisters, especially the poor ones, the ones in need, is axiomatic.

How that solidarity works out—you have prayer, you have to have outreach—is open to a variety of approaches. From deciding, like Jaroslav Vanek, to put solar energy at the service of the poor; to Dick Fratianne ministering to burn victims at the hospital; to John Butler working at Lorton prison; to Ralph Neas deciding to become involved in politics; to Pam Formica telling us something, not about her profession as a physician, but about her outreach as a neighbor; to Carol Crater deciding to become involved in a more contemplative form of ministry—all of these people say one very important thing: Action and contemplation go hand-in-hand. They are not either/ors. You do not have one group praying and one group acting; you have one group praying *and* acting. But it is very simply a matter of deciding what form our contemplation and action are going to take—how they are going to take place; everyone has a different style. I think it is enormously detrimental to expect everyone to act and contemplate in the same way. We all have special gifts of action and we all have special leadings from our contemplation and prayer life. The fact that some groups want to be more actively engaged in politics is fine for them, but it need not be your style; it need not be my style. The fact that some people want to teach is fine, but that need not be the ministry for everyone.

Speaking of work, an incarnational spirituality—the kind we are talking about with two feet in the world which is decidedly character-istic of the laity—reaffirms the intrinsic value of work. I do not know if you know this, but in the Greco-Roman world, work was regarded as vulgar. The ideal expressed in the classical tradition by Plato was basically parasitical. The gentlemen (that noun is intentionally sexist), the philosophers, and so on existed and were maintained by other people's work. The gentlemen never worked. Despite early and late attempts at social reform within the Roman Empire, the effort to grant or restore dignity to labor, especially agricultural labor, failed. But with the attainment of greater influence by Christianity, especially through the monastic movement, work began to be regarded as a consecrated activity. Biblical realism that describes the Church by a series of images, metaphors, or similes conveniently borrows from the metaphor of bread to describe what work is for the Catholic Christian. And that is what I want to suggest to all of you right now.

There is a stage initially for all of us, where the lay person— Christian, Catholic, or otherwise—decides and needs to make bread in order to support him or herself and family. Making bread—you know what that means and you know how it is used in common parlance—in the sense of earning a living, supporting a life style, widening the chasm with the have-nots, is not of itself a Christian vocation. Jesus, in fact, declined Satan's proposition: "Take these stones and make bread." Jesus said, "No." That Jesus did not do Satan's bidding is not surprising, but it is instructive; for Jesus made a curious pact with bread that tells us about the lay person's work in the world. Matthew 26:26 states, "He took bread and said, 'This is my body.' " Jesus decided not to *make* bread, but to *be* bread; he asks the same of us.

That, incidentally, is what I have heard from a lot of you in the time that we have been together. When making bread only means earning a living, supporting a life style, widening the chasm with the have-nots, there is nothing redemptive about that kind of work. But when we *are* bread for others—in the family, in the marketplace, wherever we are—when we are bread and share our daily bread, when we give ourselves, we enter the distinctively Christian vocation of living for others; the work we do becomes sanctified. Gandhi said, "There are so many hungry people in the world, if God were to appear to them God would come as bread." And it happened. But Gandhi had in mind feeding the economically poor which is a serious, critical vocation ministry for the Church.

But there are other needs that have to be fed, and sometimes we get in touch with those needs by raising people's consciousness of hungers they did not even know they had. So you have to raise people's consciousness and then feed them. The tragedy is Jesus comes as bread—as meal—and many people prefer to regard him as an hors d'oeuvre.

One more thing. Not only did Jesus come as bread, but he came as bread to be broken. He broke the bread and gave it to his disciples. In the synoptic institution narratives, Jesus is very up-front about this; and it is a crucial thing, too, for a temptation lingers for those who are bread for others to bask in the limelight and get swept away by the accolades and hosannas that go along with messiahship. If you are bread, you are in a very good position. It is heady business—being just what the people need and what the world is looking for. But in the act of offering one's life for others, of being bread broken, eaten, consumed, and used up, all bets are off for glittery fame or stardom. That kind of giving is pure, motivated by loving, death-dealing if life-yielding, and preposterously creative even in its final breath. Ernest Hemingway said, "The world breaks us all, some become strong at the broken places."

I do not have to go far to find you a role model of someone who is bread broken. I am able to choose from among the contemporary Roman Catholic laity someone we will all recognize under this symbolism of bread—Benigno Aquino. As an upper middle-class Filipino, Aquino did his share of making bread, but he also heard and followed a call to be bread for his people. Exiled in America, honored in our academic circles (when Aquino came from the Marcos regime to America, he taught at Harvard and M.I.T.), Aquino returned to Manila on August 21 of this year to again offer his gifts and energies to his brothers and sisters, to be the rallying focus of their dreams of democracy—to be bread. But he did more than that. He was willing to do more than that. For he was not naive and he knew the risks involved in his return to the Philippines. Benigno Aquino was a layperson who lived the eucharistic vocation to the end, as bread broken. Even now we have clues that this brother's life and death are still nourishing, hopefully one day healing, the people he loved.

I am not certain there is anything further I want to say about bread other than this: Costly discipleship is the name of the game and it rests at the heart of prayer. No part of our Church should encourage laity simply to make bread, even if that bread is tossed into the Sunday collection bread basket. The role models that excite us and speak to us of pressing on and pushing forward in our life with Christ are those of men and women who were not content with making bread, but who knew how to identify with it and were graced even to be bread broken as their Master was.

My last point is growth. The growth I have in mind touches on faith development, moral development, spiritual development, and full-person development.

Adult growth comes from self-knowledge, from experiences, and from reflecting on experiences. That is why we all like the talks that we have heard. People told us experiences, and they told us how they reflected on them and what they learned from them.

There is a prevailing myth that states adults learn by experiences. That is nonsense; that is precisely a myth. You learn nothing by experiences. You learn only by *reflecting* on your experiences. I will leave it to you to reflect on how well the Church has served you in growth.

We are, many of us, parents. Some of us are grandparents. With our combined track records and histories we know the delicate balance of elements needed to bring our children to responsible adulthood: timing, what Dr. Spock used to call readiness; consistency; challenge; confidence; independence; role-modeling—all offered in a supportive, affirming atmosphere where the person, not accomplishments, are valued and where (I thought of Dick's point this morning about the burn center where failure is tolerated) forgiveness is extended. This is important for growth. If failure is not tolerated in the Church, there will be no growth.

I think the Apostle Paul may have framed the most helpful discussion of Christian wholeness, hence adulthood, when he wrote of the gifts and fruits of the Spirit. This is not original with me, but I forget my original source. Paul writes of the gifts of the Holy Spirit in I Corinthians 12 and lists them. One may have the gift of preaching, another the gift of teaching, one the gift of healing, power of miracles, prophecy, recognizing spirits, ability to interpret spirits, but all these are the work of the one and the same Spirit. Paul writes of the fruits in Galatians 5. What the Spirit brings is love, joy, peace, patience, kindness, goodness, trustfulness, gentleness, and self-control. I really want you to hear those fruits again: love, joy, peace, patience, kindness, goodness, trustfulness, gentleness, and self-control. For Paul, the whole person was a person who had a gift and combined it with fruits: the healer who was kind and patient, the preacher who was honest and joyful, the prophet who exercised self-control and goodness. That is the whole person model.

It sounds good. It sounds ideal, in fact—in theory. In practice, however, this is not how it evolves. For in practice, it frequently occurs that the gifts are separated from the fruits, with the gifts being attributed to the clergy, and the fruits becoming the specialty of the laity. The whole Church is not perceived as clergy with gifts, however. There are segments of the Church—pockets of the Church—where this division of gifts and fruits is experienced. If you do not experience this division—as I do not always experience it—you feel you are in a Church that is enabling you to grow. If you do experience the division, these words put a handle on your experience. So the clergy are the ones with the gifts, and the laity are the ones with the fruits, and that is whole Church presented to people. That is not whole Church. When a highly gifted clergy selects a lay person who excels as a fruit to come into that mix, that is not whole Church either. One-half person and one-half person do not a whole person make.

Suffice it to say that there is little hope for growth, either for clergy or laity, which is to say Church, when this happens. I do not have to tell you that such was not the case with this consultation. I know you know that. But it does seem appropriate to call your attention to the superb document that was sent to each of you, published by the National Conference of Catholic Bishops three years ago, titled *Called and Gifted: The American Catholic Laity*. That is the crux of it, you see. *The Gifts Reader*, another publication not sent to you but on our reading list, published by the Bishops' Committee on the Laity just this year, is also worth noting. Fidelity to that insight, that laity are gifted as well as fruited, is the hope of the Church. The bishops seem to know that, and we ought to applaud them for knowing it.

If the model, then, of Christian wholeness is the person who combines gifts and fruits, I would still have to say a final word about how growth for that person occurs. It happens through prayer, which provides each of us the opportunity of touching base with God's love. I think of Dick's statement this morning; I think he said it all: We are ultimately made for nothing but love, to love and be loved worthily with fidelity for ever. Most of us have dabbled and dared in loves which blow hot and cold, teasing, coaxing, playing games with us, tossing us off balance, promising undeliverable goods, so that when we come upon the love of God for us and sense the simple and severe quality of it all—the honesty, openness, evenness, abandon—we know we are in a different league altogether.

In prayer and only in prayer, we find a love affair that approximates, yet exceeds, the best of our earthly loves. It is in prayer we are invited, indeed compelled, by God's love of the beauty that God sees in us to become the beauty that we are, and so become ourselves. Love is both cause and occasion of growth. Notice how that model of growth approximates a spring bubbling from an underground source—the Holy Spirit—to sustain, nourish, and refresh us, rather than the model of growth sometimes experienced outside of prayer—that of plants being watered by the hierarchy. In prayer, all are fed by the internal spring of the Holy Spirit, laity and hierarchy alike. All surrender eventually, and in varying degrees, to the same Holy Spirit. All come to know the movement of that Spirit pointing to Christ and all of them know new life in Christ.

Without a doubt it would be in the best interest of the Church not to decline the laity an opportunity to grow and live as they feel called through their relationship with the Lord. And it would be in the best interests of us all, for the sake of our spiritual health and well-being, our identity, growth, and our work, that we keep nourished by prayer.

After all, what does it profit a person if he or she has a bell, and a mirror, and a ladder, and a swing, and forgets the bird seed? The Gospel says such a person will not make it across the finish line.

Thank you.

Questions for Reflection

1. Dr. Donnelly speaks of the gift of transparency—of letting the ego get out of the way. Do you ever experience God's life and being shining through you and through what you do? What are the occasions? Can you name someone who has reached this stage of transparency? What is it about this person that makes you feel he or she has the gift of transparency?

_____

_____

_____

_____

_____

2. In the spiritual journey, there are four major stages: (1) very large ego, centered; (2) somewhat reduced ego, still centered; (3) reduced ego, decentered; (4) death of ego/birth of real self, beginning of transparency. At what stage are you in your own spiritual journey? How have you reached this stage? What preparations are you making for the continuation of your journey?

_____

_____

_____

_____

_____

3. In Matthew 26:26, Jesus takes bread and says, "This is my body." He decided not to *make* bread, as Satan bid, but rather to *be* bread. In this sense, what is the difference between making bread and being bread? Between being bread and being bread, broken? Dr. Donnelly uses Benigno Aquino as an example of a contemporary person who chose to *be* bread, broken. Can you name some other contemporaries who *are* bread? Why?

The World Today and Tomorrow
Its Meaning for the Church

Rev. John A. Coleman, SJ

The story is told about a sultan who asked a soothsayer to predict his future for him. The soothsayer looked at the globe and said, "Sire, I have great news. All your relatives will die before you." And the sultan was exceedingly angry and called in his retainers and he said, "Kill that man, the bearer of bad news."

Then he called in a second soothsayer and again asked that he predict his future. This second soothsayer looked into the globe and said, "Sire, I have great news for you. You will outlive all your relatives." And the sultan said, "Reward that man."

You will notice that the predictions are exactly the same, but that the tone is different.

I have been asked to look at the globe and address the impossibly grandiose and vague topic of the world, today and tomorrow, and its meaning for the Church. Even though I am a Jesuit, believe it or not I am not that pretentious! In fact, I wondered why I was invited here. I am not a layman, but probably because I am a Jesuit they think I am secular enough to talk about it.

For some time I have been searching for a tone to give these predictions about the world today and tomorrow (and the Church today and tomorrow) which might help our discussions here. In fact, from time to time, I have been giggling, because I have a friend I live with, a young Jesuit graduate student. He is very brilliant; he has read everything. His specialty is hermeneutics, the theory of interpretation. He reads practically every book and all the learned journals. He speaks like a review in the *New York Review of Books*. He has been taking a long time doing graduate studies, and his provincial—knowing his brilliance but worrying about whether he would ever finish his degree—began to press him on whether he had begun to narrow down his interests to some topic that was researchable in a rigid and narrow kind of way for a dissertation. My friend answered his provincial, and with the answer that provincial's face dropped. He said, "Yes, indeed. I have given lots of thought to that. I have a rigid and researchable topic. It is the world."

Perhaps it might be best to share what Dolores Leckey wrote to me on May 25 in order to give you a sense of the kinds of questions and rhetorical topics which the consultation's planners had in mind for this presentation. I quote from that letter.

"The main focus of your talk, as we envision it, would be your reflections, insights on the trends in the many systems which are now shaping our lives, the context for all of our ministries. The underlying question is *what kind of ministry is needed now and in the future to enable busy lay people, committed to secular vocations, to be consciously Christian and in the world?* The key words are secular, Christian, complexities of lay life, the future, the ministry."

Yesterday Tony Downs was telling us about things he was sure of and things he was not so sure of. I am less than sure that what I am going to do this morning will be the best way of construing these topics for this discussion. You will have to judge that yourselves. But I am terribly sure and I am terribly comfortable that these underlying questions about the world and future—the context for our ministry, whatever that is—about secular and Christian at the same time, in the world and Christian at the same time, are absolutely essential for serious attempts at pastoral life in the Church in the modern world. I have decided to focus on only two of these topics and, depending on time, I may only really develop one in length. I will state some propositions or questions, because I really come with questions rather than answers about each.

The first has to do with the constellation world/future and the second about the constellation secular and Christian—Christian in the world. If you are like me you need headlines so I am going to give you the headlines, and if you find them interesting you might read the story and listen; if not, you can doze off. But you will know what is coming anyway.

First, concerning the constellation world/future, my general proposition will be the following: The world, or at least an important segment in our world (in the secular world), has been giving a great deal of thought to the future, much more than we have as Church. What I am referring to here is the kind of project that was started in 1968 by the Rand Corporation, which was picked up by Daniel Bell and the Commission Toward the Year 2000 in the mid-1960s, the Club of Rome Report, the Brandt Report, the futurable projects in France around Bertrand de Jouvenel, and of course the Global 2000 Report that was commissioned by President Carter for the Department of State. What these things have generally been interested in, in a profound way, is discerning the trends of the times (perhaps if we want to use biblical language you might even say the signs of the times) and identifying those problems we will surely have to face, those problems that are not going to go away. Some of them are more careful about saying, "We are not sure at this point, it may be premature to say, well, this is the only solution, but what are the problems that are going to be on the agenda for the world in the future." And, therefore, for the Church.

Generally, what is quite interesting if you do a review of this genre of literature, futurology, is that they do not think much about us—the churches—when they do their futurology. They are not anti-Church, but no attention is paid. There is almost nothing about religion in these reports. Somehow they imagine the future without seeing the Church, and I want to press that in the first part of the question. Why?

My second headline, which will be the second part, and depending on time it will be developed at greater or lesser length, is about the constellation secular, in the world and Christian at the same time. I think we are really naive about the complexities of that—what people have asked us to do is to find what it means in ordinary and everyday life to have a spirituality that comes out of living in the secular world. Well, it is very difficult. But if we could achieve that spirituality in the world, we would be achieving much more than something that is really important for Catholics or Christians. It is essential for the future of our world, and I want to develop that point.

In recent years—headline number one about the future—people have been thinking about the future and trying to discern the trends of the times in order to tell us what context the world is going to have to deal with, what the Church is going to have to deal with, but generally they do not think very much of Church. It does not enter into their calculations.

Many studies have attempted to project alternative scenarios concerning the probable stage of global justice as we enter the twenty-first century, taking into account projections of probable population increase, food capacity, known energy sources, and environmental pollution. Each of these studies—such as the Club of Rome Report, the Brandt Report, the World Order Project, the Commission Toward the Year 2000 of the American Academy of Sciences in the 1960s, and the Global 2000 Report to President Carter which was commissioned by the Council on Environmental Quality and the Department of State— each of these studies has engaged mainline economists, political scientists, demographers, and politicians, and in many cases also physicists, geneticists, and so forth. They have engaged them in long-range estimates, based on projections of current trends and models, of the prospects of global prosperity and justice by the turn of the century. Each report, of course, is fallible and subject to debate and revision. Within this kind of genre of writing about the future, there has actually been a growing sophistication about this sort of thing.

In particular, taking trends that we find right now and simply projecting them into the future in a kind of naive way is quite dangerous since they may be overturned. By that, I mean demographic aspects might be overturned slightly. Or, simply projecting the trends does not tell us the causal connections between them. Some of the trends might be at counter purposes, so you have to be careful in making projections. More and more of the people engaged in this area are becoming a little more humble about what they are doing. None can foresee all future contingencies, surely. Still with all their failings, methodological as well as other kinds—some of the economists and others in this room could speak to this better than I—it seems to me that these kinds of reports which are trying to discern the trends of the times, trying to tell us what the problems are that are not going to go away easily between now and the twenty-first century, strike me as providing us with the best working data against mere denial. (I will come back to that point—the tendency of people when faced with bad news to say kill the man: denial.) These reports also provide data against mere wishful thinking (somehow we will get a little gadget tomorrow that will take all these problems away). It seems to me that these reports provide us with the best working data for predicting the next several decades; they are an exercise—or attempt to be an exercise, however imperfect methodologically—in what we might call prudence, planning, and responsibility.

The remarkable fact is that there is an extraordinary convergence of all these studies and their judgments which we are facing, as a world—severe new limits of scarcity that will tax the very caring capacity and sustainability of the planet Earth. None of the reports presents rosy or optimistic pictures of the human future, although some are more pessimistic than others. All predict that the large existing gap between the rich and poor nations will likely widen. If you want the most dismal view of this, you can read economist Robert Heilbroner's book, *The Human Prospect*, where he talks about scarcity and the growing gap between the rich and poor nations, the possibility of nuclear blackmail, the rise of authoritarian governments as setting a pattern throughout most of the world (the 70 to 80 percent of the population which is called the Third and Fourth Worlds), and perhaps, he thought, even some authoritarian religion to bolster that. Heilbroner's outlook is the most dismal. Several others predict severe famines—and, after all that is already happening—and large-scale starvation of millions of humans in the Third World, especially Asia, by the first decade of the next century. As the Global 2000 Report puts it: If present trends continue—and maybe they will not, but we do not have any reason now to see why they are not going to—the world in 2000 will be more crowded, more polluted, less stable ecologically, and more vulnerable to disruption than the world we live in now. Serious stresses involving population resources and environment are clearly visible ahead. Despite greater material output—it will be increased—the world's people will be poorer in many ways than they are today. That is the prediction.

It is instructive to compare best-case and worst-case scenarios. One of the things these projectionists try to do is say, well, here is a trend. It appears that we do not have any reason to believe that there is a quick-fix for any of these things; on the basis of that we are making some predictions that will be open to revision, and we are going to play with some models about worst-case/best-case scenarios.

Even the best-case scenario, which is that we will survive with perhaps a minimum of dignity but with increasing problems, assumes the need for complex, long-term cooperation and planning to begin now. It is especially instructive to look at the assumptions necessary to make a best-case scenario possible. Several citations from the Global 2000 Report will make the point.

"These problems are inexorably linked to some of the most perplexing and persistent problems of the world: (there is no easy fix) poverty, injustice and social conflict. New and imaginative ideas and a willing-ness to act on them are essential. The needed changes go far beyond the capability and responsibility of this or any other single nation. An era of unprecedented cooperation and commitment is essential."

Throughout these various futurists' projections which forecast likely population increases, water, timber and mineral resources, food pro-duction, and environmental carrying capacity for the year 2000, every best-case scenario assumes that even the most minimal global justice—and what we mean by this is providing the bare, minimal, basic human needs in terms of food and health systems for mere survival, let alone flourishing—is possible only, as the Global 2000 Report puts it, assum-ing (what an assumption) there are no disastrous wars, famine, or pestilence. Yet, the report goes on to remind us that the world will be more vulnerable to the destructive effects of war. The tensions that could lead to war will have multiplied. The potential for conflict, for example, over fresh water alone is underscored by the fact that out of 200 of the world's major rivers, 148 are shared by two countries—source of tension and possible war, as water becomes a very important resource—and fifty-two are shared by three to ten countries, so one thinks of the Plata (Brazil/Argentina), the Euphrates (Syria/Iraq), and the Ganges (Bangladesh/India); and over this conflicts could easily intensify.

Now without being clear what program to espouse to deal with these problems, the Global 2000 Report reminds us of problems that simply will not go away, which include important justice issues, and which call for new and imaginative solutions and resources for cooperation and commitment on issues such as transfer of trade, of capital—human and other kinds of capital—and technology, issues of peace, develop-ment, the North-South debate, issues of energy sources and issues of security against war and terrorism. These are the issues with which we are going to struggle.

There is a strong sense of denial when faced with unpleasant facts. We are all human; the first thing we do when we find out we are going to die is to deny it. There is a strong tendency to denial, to avoid the issue until it is too late—or, the opposite of that, to wishful thinking.

I saw that in Bolivia this summer when I was in Latin America which is in awful shape. No one knows a really best-case scenario for Bolivia. There is a strong man there somewhere in the military who is strong and honest. He is going to come, or there is a gadget somewhere.

Boy! We have this one gadget that will solve all our problems. Now against that what we need as a world, it seems to me, is a virtue called realism with hope. And I am going to suggest that is going to be the role of religion. I was quite taken yesterday with Richard Fratianne's use of compassion without pity and love without sentimentality. I liked it because it was a secular statement, really, of deep Christian values. So I want to talk about a secular statement of deep Christian values. Realism with hope; that is what our world needs.

Note that the report that I am referring to here, the Global 2000 Report, did not seem to feel that it was necessary to say anything about religion as a possible resource for dealing with any of these important and life-shaping issues. Why?

A second report was a bit more rosy, although it is still the same message. But the sultan might not say immediately, "Kill us." It is interesting; it comes from the 1960s, although it is still instructive reading today, I think. I am referring to the famous Daniel Bell Report of the Commission Toward the Year 2000 done in the 1960s by the American Academy of Arts and Sciences. It is impossible to summarize the far-ranging discussion of social scientists, physicists, engineers, and political figures who contributed to this report. Here, however, it might be helpful just to list the kinds of questions which arose. They were being very careful about saying, "We are not going to look for a solution. It is too soon. But what are the problems that we are going to have to deal with?" They listed them under four general areas. Let me just give you a sense of them without going into any detail: technological changes, psychological and sociological problems, political problems, and economic and demographic problems.

They recognized with humility that if you had asked a group of scientists in 1880 what was going to be the most important technological innovation in the next fifty years, probably none of them would have predicted the X-ray. So that, clearly, we are not very good about predicting certain possible technological innovations. Something wonderful may happen, although it is not likely that something wonderful will be a cheap-fix for all of these problems. But facing that, they focused basically on the technology that we already know about. And raised questions not about "achieving the gadget," but about the social and political ramifications of the gadget. And, of course, they talked about automation, robots, and about information technology, especially the social impact of the computer.

You see, it was one thing to invent the automobile; it was quite another thing to imagine what the social impact would be when you have a network of highways. You created a national market that was not there before. You had impact on the family system with new mobility, problems of pollution, and so forth. It is that kind of question they want to raise—the computer questions about patterns of work and leisure, about access or non-access. Now, the computer is a very powerful thing. It has information; information is power. It provides access and non-access, and therefore will determine the new elites, and those who are going to be left out—which is of course the justice issue.

When I was in Latin America, I heard a lot of people say, "We will never be part of the game. This is the new game for global, economic, political, cultural issues; we will never be part of this game. We are left out." They also paid attention to biomedical sciences and technology, genetic engineering and so forth. So, issues of technological changes are important.

Issues of psychological and sociological changes are also important, and here history was very instructive. After all, in the Industrial Revolution of the nineteenth century we had the invention of two things. The first was childhood. There were children before, but never childhood. After all, remember the stories of Dickens—children went to work at age seven. The second was adolescence. We had amazing social repercussions connected with that—the rise of education. Everyone went to school in the nineteenth century—very few did before that time—and with the availability of education came all its implications: creation of a new mobility, creation of more democratic opportunities for learning, and so forth.

With that historical example in mind, people were starting to talk about issues of changes in the life cycle, at least in the First World. People are now living into their seventies. Theresa Sullivan, a demographer at the University of Chicago, pointed out "till death do us part" meant something quite different in the nineteenth century when the average length of a marriage was eleven to fifteen years. People died young. Well, one would say, " 'Till death do us part'—I could put up with fifteen years." Yet the likelihood is that it is now going to be fifty years. That demographic change is one of enormous psychological and sociological significance. Another important change occurred with the expansion of career opportunities. It was one thing when one prepared for a career for life and quite another when one could have multiple careers. So the demographers looked at those problems.

Along with the average citizen's increased life span came a range of political problems: density, overcrowding, and issues of public planning. A vast expansion of social regulation—by the state or by other agencies—was assumed. And with that expansion came a whole set of problems, including not only the problems themselves, but the ways in which we conceptualized them.

What I found quite interesting was the general agreement among those nineteenth century social scientists who were engaged in economy—or the dismal science, as it was called—that the prevailing concept of social justice (based on individualism, a social contract, the protection of negative liberties of individuals, individual preference, and balance of interest) would need to be thought through again because of the new role of the state and other planning and scaling and zoning and controlling agencies in the world. As they put it, "We need a deep change in our understanding of social justice because the one we have received was inherited from a very different world—the beginning of the nineteenth century—and it is not a good description of what we are really doing. It does not help us very much in dealing with issues of social justice in this changed setting."

And finally, under economic and demographic problems there were the obvious ones of population, new food and energy sources, and trade and technology transfers. Again, what I found very enlightening was the general agreement of the social scientists to the following proposition: Some new philosophy is necessary to guide society in the twenty-first century.

These people, it occurred to me, were basically careful and generally humble about what they were doing. They methodologically recognized the notorious problems in mirror projections of trends—assuming that you simply take the ongoing agenda of 1983 and project it into the future, that is rather stupid—or the limitation of certain economic and logical models which do not include relevant data or questions. They all agreed that at some point we also needed what they call normative models—not simply projections based on statistical trends, not simply logical and economic models that talk about causal factors—that would point to the kinds of things we want to do, whatever the trends. What values would we not want to see eroded? What values would we want to protect, whatever the trends? Or at least, what values would we want to protect, inasmuch as possible, against the trends? As Erik Erikson stated in his characteristic wisdom, "One can undertake to predict only on the basis of one or two premises: Either one expects that things will be as bad as they have always been, only worse, or one visualizes what one is willing to take a chance on at the risk of being irrelevant." Your normative models would be attempting to isolate that.

Once again I note the almost complete absence of any theological voices in the Daniel Bell Commission Toward the Year 2000 (Krister Stendahl did a little coda, but he was not part of the conversation; it was to make the Commission look respectable). Nor was any attention paid to the churches, and by this I do not mean bishops or theologians, but rather the churches themselves and what resources they might bring to the normative models of motivation, symbolic hope, or ethical wisdom.

Why was there an absence of Church? As one goes through this material on projections, somehow the future is being thought of with no attention being paid to the churches or to religion. Why does this absence of Church exist?

I would suggest several reasons. One reason may be due to a myopia of the secular intellectual establishment about religion; they are just blind to it. That certainly plays some role. One reason will be made in my next point about secularity and being Christian in a secular world, and so I will postpone it. But the other reason is that these are not the kinds of questions which are foremost on church agendas, although the *Decree on the Apostolate of Lay People* of the Second Vatican Council speaks of the need for study sessions, congresses, periods of recollection, frequent meetings, conferences, books, and periodicals which would address the role of the laity in the world of work and the temporal sphere. Such aids are few and far between, and to the best of my knowledge—now I may be wrong, but I try to follow the national Catholic Church as best I can—the last consultation on the laity on the national level was held here in Notre Dame in 1979— hardly frequent meetings. The fact that our agenda for this consultation is very diffuse reflects that we are only beginning; we are brainstorming; we are in the formative stage.

In the debate about future policy, which is going to continue, specialists and generalists will be pitted against one another as in the past. The debate is between the knowledge experts and those who are more generalists. But we ought to pay attention to who these generalists tend to be. The generalists who will make a difference in these debates will press the issues of value, the underlying conception of justice, distributive justice and human dignity. After all, what are these people talking about? They are talking about some profound, new way of imagining society; some profound, new concept of social justice. This is not norm-free. This is not simply left to the technical experts.

In the debate there will be specialists and generalists, but who are the generalists that will make a difference in this kind of debate? They are not going to be theologians, by and large; and I will give you a reason why. If you spend a lot of time in secular academia, or if you read the *New York Review of Books* or whatever, how is the word "theology" used? It is always a pejorative term. What does it mean? It means one of two things: coming in from the outside with judgments that might be interesting but do not seem to have arisen from within the secular milieu itself, or scholastic hair-splitting about something. At University of California conferences, whenever the word theology is used, that is what it means. So, the debate between the specialists who are narrow without spirit and without vision, and the generalists who are pushing the issues of human dignity and justice and so forth, will be between the specialists and those generalists who know enough about the specialists' issues that they can address the ethical, moral, and religious issues from within the secular milieu itself. And those generalists are going to be from the laity.

I will give you three examples that immediately come to mind of generalists who are making a difference—a profound difference—in these debates about policy and the future.

One example is a man named Freeman Dyson at Princeton University, who has written a very interesting and beautiful book called *Disturbing the Universe*, which raises questions about science, technology, and society. There are two interesting things about Freeman Dyson. First of all, he was a specialist—after all he worked with Teller and others. He is also a profoundly religious man; we see, I think, that it is from that religious background—his Quaker religious background—that the sense of pressing values, of working from within the world, the specialized domain of science and technology, and pressing issues about human dignity and justice come.

Another generalist candidate for me would be George Kennan. Again, he is a generalist pressing religious and other kinds of values in ways that are making a difference to the narrow, specialized debate. George Kennan is an Episcopal layman.

A third example is someone I know personally, Herbert York at the University of California, San Diego, who is a physicist, and former head of Livermore Lab. He has been deeply pressing value questions in terms of technology and the arms race. Herbert York is also an Episcopal layman.

It is interesting to me that all three examples show some kind of religious background. The people who are going to make the Church effective on issues that are clearly normative value issues that touch at the heart, the meaning of the human and the social for the future, will be those kinds of people who, from within the secular milieu itself, can ask the questions and push the value judgments. Otherwise, it is going to seem like it is from the outside.

I have given some broader examples of sciences, but it seems to me that if we are really going to push the understanding of medical, legal, and business ethics—to take more homely examples within institutional life—it is going to be, once again, a debate between the specialists and the generalists. The generalists are going to be those who have been part of that milieu and bring the values out of religious nurturance.

I was reading The New York Times recently—I have talked about a doomsday agenda—and discovered a wonderful headline. It was in conjunction with an interview on the president of the Club of Rome, and the headline was "Doomsday Agenda Bears Hope." Now it strikes me that the churches carry within themselves, rather uniquely, a deep combination of what I want to call realism—believing in God does not mean there is not going to be a doomsday agenda or that there will not be concentration camps or that there will not be war or whatever—a deep realism because of our understanding of sin, as well as a recognition that, however bad the situation, there is always something more human within it. That is what God means. There is always something more than just faith. And it seems to me the important nurturance of the Church will be to provide that for our laity. We deeply need that kind of person on the agenda.

Now not all secular social scientists have been negative in their understanding of religion. One whom I admire deeply, Sheldon Wolin, has made the following remark: "The historical contribution of Western religions to the political education of ordinary people in their work world, and poor people, is almost impossible to exaggerate. Religion supplied a first-hand experience of what it meant to be a member of a community, what it meant to sacrifice and to share, to be empowered, to make not just promises but commitments of long duration, and to refuse to conform for conscience's sake. And, not least, to found new communities." Now that is a description of what religion has done, I think, in the political education of ordinary people and the history of Western society.

It seems to me that many of the things that Wolin is pointing out are precisely the virtues that we are going to need as we face this agenda of the future. We are going to need people who can imagine and have experienced real community in societies that find that difficult—first-hand experiences of what it is to be a member of a community. But what if we churches are not providing that? Then we are not nurturing the kind of lay imagination that can make an impact on the world. So, if we are not providing that sense of community, we are not nurturing this contribution.

We are going to need people who can recognize the need to sacrifice and share with hope; to not only make promises that are just, but commitments of a long duration, which after all is what all this futurology is about, to refuse to conform for conscience's sake, and—not the least—to found new communities.

So as far as my own reading of this, there is a major role for the Church to play in this agenda of the future. But it is really preconditioned on the Church providing, in the lives of our ordinary Catholics, a first-hand experience of what it is to be a member of a community of sharing and sacrifice. When that becomes a description and not simply our ideal type, then the Church will have an indispensable role as the bearer (to use your phrase) of the revolution of the heart—not necessarily the barricades—that will be essential if we are going to face the agenda for the twenty-first century with realism, against all of the temptations to mindless denial or wishful thinking, as well as with hope.

My second point is related to what I just said, but it is not, simply the same by further examples. I want to play with this theme of being Christians in a secular world—a worldly vocation, a vocation to transform this world—not fleeing the world, or protecting ourselves from it, or giving ourselves easy outs like, "That is only secular humanism, that is bad. We will protect ourselves."

I think being Christians in a secular world is far more difficult and far more of a challenge than we are really prepared to admit. The Second Vatican Council, you know, was rather naive on the issue of secularity. It was reacting to its own past where it simply condemned the secular, so it then tended to affirm it, somewhat one-dimensionally. Even at the time, secular observers or Protestant observers all pointed that out, and especially at the point in time when the very meaning of secularity was beginning to crumble.

In paragraph three of the *Decree on the Apostolate of Lay People* of Vatican II, it recognizes the rightful world of the secular. In talking about a spirituality for work and life in a secular world, that decree notes a preference for spirituality which shows "a closer harmony between the everyday life of the members and their faith." People here at this consultation have been talking about that—everyday life, ordinary life, and a harmony between that and their faith.

The decree also notes the distinctively secular quality of the lay state and its own form of spirituality—not a monastic spirituality, but its own form—that will be close to the world of everyday life. My question is, What is that form to be and why is it important not simply to help Christian laity in the world, but for our wider world?

Obviously this lay spirituality, this lay vocation, will include common Christian elements of discernment, fidelity to God, prayer, charity, and vocation. By the way, I do not think it is helpful to speak of a vocation to the lay state, anymore than I think that it is healthy simply to speak in general of vocation to priesthood without talking about ministry within that person. But what seems clear to me is that the vocation is always to some definite task and mission, to some gift and charism in the lay state. Whatever lay spirituality will be, it will be incarnational. It will recognize that the social world constitutes some God-given testing ground to be lived through and confronted, not avoided.

I would like to refer to a recent set of essays which appeared first in the "Daedalus Journal" about a year ago and then as a book, *Religion in America,* subtitled "Spirituality in a Secular Age." The essays are mainly written by several social scientists and worldly intellectuals, and not by theologians, although Martin Marty and several church historians contributed some very thoughtful pieces.

Despite wide divergence on many issues, there was, nevertheless, consensus by these authors that American religion, and religion in the

First World at any rate, is increasingly privatistic, secularistic, or nostalgic. One author put it this way: "Our contemporary religious situation is characterized by two tendencies that are part of advanced modernity and secularity. The first is the tendency of modern culture to treat the religious world view as a partial one and to make religion subjective. And the second is the tendency of modern society to de-politicize institutional religion, to privatize it, and to specify its social function in such a way that it serves the exclusive purpose of inter-preting and organizing the relation of human beings to the sacred."

Now what he is saying effectively is the modern world has separate domains, and it does not have a way of conceiving the possibility—in fact denies it—or the legitimacy of putting religion and economics, religion and politics, or religion in the world of everyday life together. One of the difficulties we find in doing this is not because we have not been pastorally imaginative—looking for a gimmick to do this—but because to try to do this is a profoundly countercultural act.

In this same context, Louis Dupre of Yale University has a very thoughtful essay called "Spiritual Life in a Secular Age." Dupre describes the modern world as one that conceives of life as not reconciled and not integrated and not *capable* of that. It is divided into domains, each with its own laws: economics, politics, family, law, religion, everyday life. Part of this modern situation of secularity is the eclipse of any strong, special sacred sense of transcendence. Dupre claims the sacred, wherever it is still experienced, has lost the power to integrate directly the rest of life. No mere gimcrack program will solve this problem. And there is no quick-fix of how we are going to pray that will do it. The modern world in its own self-conception—and I think if we described it, we would say this is also true—does not hold together. There is a collapse of any integrating vision and the inability, really, to hold it together. Instead it looks more like a supermarket of choice, pluralism, and information overload.

Dupre points out that in the face of secularity and the collapse of any integrating vision, many people in our society are turning toward inward life, toward issues of spirituality, as a strategy of survival and as a kind of protest against the shallowness of a closed, secular world. The revival of spirituality in Catholicism in the last few years goes hand-in-hand with the revival, outside the churches, with the move-ment toward the new religious movements and even toward secular forms of spirituality.

In Berkeley I am in a conference at the Institute of Human Development with people who do not believe in God but are very interested in spirituality. What are they interested in? They are interested in the following. They have seen that this modern world view, the secular, has led to one-dimensional understanding. They have seen the shallowness and emptiness of this. They are looking for the following things. They are looking for the places in ordinary experience (they are not looking for some god who is going to come from the outside), where the ordinary invitation will be to stop for a moment, to pause. Ken Woodward was using some words for us—words to make us wonder, to make us say, "Oh, at this point I have come to the limit of my secular understanding. I am not sure." You are not into God yet, but you are some place very important where you are getting symptoms of transcendence, where you have to stop. Here there is a paradox. The models that we are using for thinking about ordinary life are breaking down. That is what the people at the Institute are looking for.

Now in this context, then, I would like to suggest that the issue of lay spirituality in the world has something to do with the quest—if I can use a good Jesuit word—of finding God in all things. But in doing that, as a Jesuit I have really wrestled with this for many years, how do I know I am finding God and not just projecting him? How will I know that I am really discovering the surprising God? We know God is at work in all creation, but somehow we think we already know how. How do I know God's presence in ordinary experiences—in a pub, for example, in life and death situations within a family, or in work situations? When there is some experience that I can point to that is breaking my ordinary categories, I may actually be finding God in all things and not simply projecting him.

Often enough, I think, when we contemplate faith in everyday life, what we are thinking about is how are we going to shore up our Christians, give them a sense that they have already met Christ, and so forth and then encourage them to go out and proof-test it in their ordinary lives. This is the challenge of spirituality in a way that none of the classics of mysticism explains. Where is God in work, in family, in economics, in trade union movements, in working for politics? Where are the signs of hope and possibility? Where are the signs of paradox where our ordinary understandings, our own ordinary secular concepts, break down? We need to do a lot of talking about this in forums where people are describing faith in everyday life; because, really, it is *there*, in that forum context, that we will be able to attempt to put faith and everyday life together. I would suggest that this is a project that is important, not just for our Christians, but for many others. This is a countercultural project but also one in which many people in this society are engaged.

As Louis Dupre tries to suggest, whatever contemplation is going to mean in our own time, in some sense you are not going to be able to appeal to a god of the gaps. You are not going to be able to appeal to another world. Contemplation is going to be of this world. What is it in our human experience that forces us to try to use religious language, even if we might be using that language too cheaply? It is not that we already know who Christ is; it is not that we already know what the will of God is. We know that God is active in the world, but why do we assume we know *how* he is active in the world?

The project of a lay spirituality which I am suggesting is not as easy as we thought it would be—no cheap-fix will do it. If our Catholic press does not publish accounts of people talking about lay spirituality, if our parishes do not help people to talk about prayer in everyday life, then little will be accomplished. This is a new kind of dialog; no one really knows how to enter into it. This type of dialogue could transform our whole society, because if we did talk about this, a truly secular and a truly Christian spirituality ultimately promises closer harmony with the world of everyday life and our faith.

We will be working often enough with secular images in this self-understanding, but with a new edge. We will be trying to point to what it is in ordinary reality—both holy and worldly—that contains limits, paradoxes, and deaths that invite further exploration from our experience of that reality. It does not come from something we already know—we already know Christ saved everyone—and it does not come from superimposing an expectation on it. What is it in family, work, and in the world of community and politics that presents an image of hope and the possibility of new ways of wholeness—a secular image, but with a new edge?

I would suggest that if this could be achieved, not only would the frustration that Christian people feel regarding this problem of prayer and spirituality in the daily world be bridged a bit, but also a new wholeness might be achieved by them. Indeed it might also have wider resonance within our diverse culture. For ultimately, if the Church exists for the world, it would be irresponsible to provide a spirituality

for Christians—for lay Christians or any Christians—that was unre-
lated to the varied spiritual quests of others in our culture.

I have made two points. There is a future. It has set our agenda,
whether we are in or out of institutions. We need realism and hope.
The Church has a role to play in meeting that need, but clearly the
key actors are the laity.

This challenge of a lay spirituality that puts together faith and the
world of everyday life is not a matter of simple gimmicks. It is a deep
challenge, an invitation to have people really share their experience
and explore that experience, so that we might find God and not simply
project him. What is the Church's ministry to the laity? It is to help
them in this process, and to support them in every way. This is
important, not simply for our Christians in the modern world, but also
for our modern world. It is part of the laity's vocation to transform the
world, and this spirituality contributes to that vocation. Thank you.

Questions for Reflection

1. The Daniel Bell Report of the Commission Toward the Year 2000 lists
four major problem areas impacting the world of tomorrow. Fr. Coleman gives
some examples of how these areas will affect us all in the coming years. Do
you agree with his assessment? What examples can you think of? As a Christian, what values can you bring to a future agenda that might not be present
in a strictly secular viewpoint?

_____

_____

_____

_____

_____

_____

2. According to Sheldon Wolin, Western religions have made considerable historical contributions to the political education of ordinary people and to the poor people of the world. Can you think of some contemporary contributions? Fr. Coleman contends that the Church has a major role to play in the agenda of the future. He gives you his interpretation of what it is. Do you agree with him? How would you define the Church's role? How well do you feel the Church is meeting the challenge of this role?

---

3. What would you answer to the following provocative questions posed by Fr. Coleman with regard to lay spirituality and being Christian in a secular world?

How do I know I am finding God in all things and not just projecting him?

How do I know God's presence in ordinary experiences?

Where is God in work, in family, in economics, in trade union movements, in working for politics?

_____

_____

_____

_____

_____

What is it in family, in work, and in the world of community and politics that presents an image of hope and the possibility of new ways of wholeness?

_____

_____

_____

_____

_____

Laity's Recommendations
to Church Leaders

Approximately fifty recommendations emerged from the "Work and Faith" consultation. Although the recommendations from the eleven groups of participants were never prioritized or formally endorsed by the whole assembly, they have been compiled by the Bishops' Committee on the Laity and utilized in publications and at subsequent meetings. Given the wide diversity among the consultation's participants, there is a remarkable convergence of opinion in their recommendations; we have broken these down into five major categories.

1. Foster dialog on work and faith. This is by far the strongest recommendation from all of the groups. The dialog begun in the national consultation should continue on national, diocesan, and parish levels. Specific suggestions include the establishment of various networks: national and local structures to foster such dialog; forums for discerning the moral dimensions of issues pertaining to work and faith; support groups for Christian workers conscious of their social mission; and liturgical and educational opportunities to examine the social teachings of the Church. Such structures and networks are needed to promote dialog between the faithful and their ministers; to foster a spirituality for lay mission; to develop a theology of work; and to assist Christians who disagree to dialog critically with each other and discover their common faith.

2. Nurture Christian community. The word *community* is often repeated in the recommendations. It mostly refers to the desire for face-to-face relationships among Christian worshipers; but it also refers to the felt need for establishing small communities in those parishes that are too large to foster a keen sense of belonging, commitment, and dialog. Some recommendations also elaborate on the urgency of community in relation to the modern family's need for communal support.

3. Promote the equality of women. These recommendations focus on the role of women in both the Church and the workplace. Movements supporting equality in the workplace should be encouraged. Church ministries should be open to both men and women, where possible.

4. Restructure church ministries. It is recommended that new lay ministries be established in response to new needs among people (e.g., divorced Catholics, the unemployed, immigrants, farmers threatened with foreclosure, and the poor suffering from the termination of government programs). Such ministries could be recognized by commissioning ceremonies and promoted among the catechumens and among the young people being confirmed. One recommendation even calls for the development of new leadership among laity to influence policy makers in Washington. Several recommendations suggest an expanded role for lay persons in parishes and dioceses where clerical leadership is diminishing.

5. Establish formation programs for laity. The restructuring of ministries and the promotion of lay mission in the marketplace need to be supported by formation programs. It is recommended that universities and retreat centers attend to this need.

The Bishops' Committee Reports

At the 1983 general assembly of the National Conference of Catholic Bishops, the Most Reverend James R. Hoffman, then chairman of the NCCB Laity Committee, gave the following report. He spoke on behalf of all the bishops who served on the Laity Committee at that time.

Three years have passed since this Conference approved the statement *Called and Gifted: The American Catholic Laity.* The last paragraph of that statement invited response on the calls to adulthood, holiness, ministry, and community.

To facilitate dialog on the section dealing with Christian life in the world, the Committee on the Laity sponsored a consultation at Notre Dame last month entitled "Work and Faith in Society: Catholic Perspectives." Its purpose was to listen to the experience of Catholic leaders in various occupations and to hear their reflections on the connection between faith and work.

Questions that served as a background were (1) What is my life as a professional like? What does it have to do with my faith? (2) What kind of ministry challenges and supports me as a Christian? (3) What are my expectations of the Church? How has the Church supported or failed me?

There were over sixty men and women in attendance from a variety of occupational backgrounds. Many were suggested by members of this body, and we are grateful for your collaboration in this important conference effort.

Consultation participants were not intended to be representative of the Church as a whole but were reflective of a cross section of the laity not usually found at church meetings. As one participant said, "The variety was amazing: from a rear admiral to an anti-nuke pacifist, from a farm worker union organizer to an insurance management official, with two members of Indian tribes—all wrestling with the question of how to be Catholic in today's America."

Our dialog at Notre Dame was candid, and the group was energized by its task. There was genuine love and appreciation for the Church and its role in giving participants a way of relating to life. As the consultation continued, we felt a power and intensity—in the open forums, which responded to the presentations, in the small-group reflections, and during informal conversations. There was a sense that something was aborning and a desire to be a part of it.

The first day was a time for unloading hurts and concerns. Two predominant areas were children and family, parish and liturgy. One of the poignant lines was voiced by a participant in words something like this: "The hardest job I have had as an adult has been raising my children. And, I can say—without blame but with intended objectivity—that the Church has been very little help." Among his examples were dragging teen-age youngsters to Mass and finding a dull liturgy and a poor homily.

Small-group discussion produced many recommendations, which the committee has grouped in six areas.

First, almost to a person, participants were grateful for the values and symbol system that they had received; they spoke warmly of the parish and/or school of their youth. However, they were not at all confident that we have produced a renewed Church that provides the same symbol system. Various pieces make sense, but we haven't yet found the unified whole that makes sense of real life.

Second, there was a consensus that the parish is critical. They remember the parish of their youth as a positive experience; often the contemporary parish does not meet their needs for spiritual nurturing, nor do homilies help them deal with key matters in their lives, nor does the parish fill their need for community. They see their vocation in the marketplace; they're looking for help in bringing their faith there. The Church, they said, has a responsibility to nurture their call through small Christian communities.

Third, as professionals, participants expressed a loneliness in their efforts to connect work and faith. The starting point is their daily experience—as attorney, as geneticist, as business leader, as actress—and that gives rise to the questions. We heard a plea for networking mechanisms, for mediating structures, including holding consultations like this on the local level. This consultation was not quite a call to action. It was simply an attempt to ask the question of the recipients of our diverse ministries: How are we doing? How does the Church affect your real life? At our Laity Committee meeting last evening we supported Bishop Untener in his plan to pilot a similar consultation in the Saginaw diocese.

Fourth, participants asked for a fuller development of a theology of work, as well as a spirituality of work, rooted in the concrete experience of the laity. Someone observed that if faith is connected with work, it can become a vocation and a joy; without faith it can become a drudgery.

Fifth, both men and women participants urgently called for the Church to listen to women, affirming without reservation women's place in the work world and their right to equal pay for equal or comparable work. Participants urged recognition and support systems for working women and said that when the ministries are restructured, they should reflect the equality of women. This recommendation underscores the importance of the workshop held this past weekend, sponsored by the Ad Hoc Committee on Women in Society and the Church. Finally, lay women and men are indeed a "called and gifted" people. They wish to place their wisdom and insight and experience at the service of the Gospel. Participants recommended the establishment of some permanent, active structure that would make the wisdom of lay experts available to bishops and clergy, especially when they address public issues, and that would alert the bishops to important new issues. Lay participation in decision making in the Church also needs to be a permanent element in the Church's structure.

The Church has much to gain if we find avenues for lay people to provide their intelligence, expertise, and wisdom in service to the Catholic community at all levels. What dare we dream? That the laity's voice will be listened to with respect, and that the laity will increasingly be involved in major decision making in the Church. The challenge to us as a Conference is to continue to work toward making this a reality.

II.

PRACTICALLY SPEAKING
PLANNING A CONSULTATION

Work and Faith in Society
How We Planned It

Patricia E. Davis

Interest has been expressed in the "how to" of the consultation on "Work and Faith in Society: Catholic Perspectives." In reflecting on that event, I discovered three key areas of preparation: purpose, people, and plans.

In the introduction to this handbook, Dolores Leckey explains the purpose of the consultation. Because most church-sponsored events are designed for those serving the institution, it was imperative that planners be clear about our different focus and communicate it well.

The need for clarity became apparent in the second area of preparation: people.

We had found eighty people to be a workable size for a consultation process. Of the eighty, twenty would be committee members and secretariat and ancilliary staff, leaving sixty invitees.

They were to be persons self-identified as Catholics and holding positions of responsibility and leadership in their occupations. Names surfaced in three ways: the committee and staff brainstormed; we sought suggestions from colleagues in other national offices; and each diocesan bishop was invited to submit names.

Eventually, we had information on about 1,000 people. First, we eliminated all those whose only noted credentials were "churchy" (e.g.,

"John Doe chairs the pastoral council and taught CCD for many years").

Then, we divided the remaining names into twelve occupational groups: the arts; business; education; government/politics/diplomacy; human service and nonprofit organizations; labor; law and law enforcement; media; medicine and health; military and defense; science; and sports/entertainment. Next, we narrowed the list to about ten people in each category, striving to preserve a balance in terms of region of the country, race, sex, and age. About half a dozen people in each group were sent invitations seven months prior to the consultation. Invitations, issued in the name of the committee, explained the purpose of the consultation and asked that participants be present for the entire event. We noted that grants would cover the cost of participants' room and board and help with transportation expenses for those needing assistance.

Invitees were asked to respond promptly, and most accepted. Those on back-up lists were invited in place of people who had declined.

Participants were asked to supply biographical information, and a month before the consultation, they were sent a list of attendees (including committee and staff) with professional and personal information on each. A suggested reading list was also sent to each participant.

Finally, the plans.

The place selected was the Morris Inn and Center for Continuing Education at the University of Notre Dame. A goal was to offer gracious hospitality and a comfortable meeting space with accommodations for the media.

The program received much attention. Our agenda included presentations, small-group discussion, and time for prayer and informal conversation. We tried to strike a balance between respecting the full schedules of busy people and creating an atmosphere conducive to reflection and dialog.

Post-consultation evaluations indicated participants appreciated the formal input but would have preferred fewer talks and more time devoted to general discussion following each presentation and to sharing in previously arranged, heterogeneous small groups.

Prayer was central to the consultation experience. Committee and staff held the event and participants in prayer—before, during, and after. A liturgist worked with planners, assuring a common vision that resulted in prayer services and a eucharistic liturgy that were unforgettable.

Nor was play ignored. A special highlight was a gala banquet with puppets, storytelling, and song late into the night.

"How to" Suggestions for
Dioceses and Parishes

One of the key recommendations of the participants in the consultation at the University of Notre Dame was that pastoral leaders sponsor similar events in dioceses and parishes throughout the country. This section of the handbook offers suggestions about how dioceses, parishes, and even organizations might do so. The four principles and two sample agendas offered below stem both from the experience of the national consultation and from discussion with dioceses and parishes in various parts of the country.

Principles to Remember

The following principles are a distillation of what participants said they valued the most in the "Work and Faith" consultation.

The first principle is that of listening. This is an essential element in consultation. One of the bishops said,

> . . . we as bishops need to have a deeper insight and understanding of lay Catholics in terms of family life and work situations.

This appreciation for leaders who listen was underscored by a number of participants:

> I have a much clearer sense of the vitality of our bishops as a result of observing them in a concentrated manner. I have always accepted their value; now I'm convinced of their vigor in leadership. I think that the bishops should sense that lay criticisms do not mean a lessening of our love and loyalty to the Church.

> It is good for the laity to feel that the bishops are listening—not agreeing necessarily, but listening.

Another participant envisioned the possibility that

> such consultations, if more broadly based, can develop a new model of "authority" in the Church—a listening rather than commanding authority.

The national consultation involved people from diverse backgrounds, including people who valued traditional Catholic ways and
people who wanted more experimentation. Nevertheless, not a single
objection was raised to pastoral leaders taking a listening stance. Participants seemed to agree that the Church needs leaders who can listen, as well as teach, administer, and act decisively with legitimate
authority.

Experience with work and faith gatherings suggests that planners
organize their programs on a consultation model. According to this
model, church leaders relate to the participants as resource persons
who possess information and skills, which they as leaders need for
effective pastoral planning and administration. While consultation
involves training, it is distinct from training inasmuch as its primary
goal is information gathering not information dissemination. Through
consultation, church leaders can gather data, in the form of feedback,
regarding their present strategies, critiques of their proposed plans,
alternative proposals and options, and reality tests of their perceptions
of the perspectives, opinions, and needs of the laity.

The second principle is that of storytelling. When asked about the
personally most rewarding aspect of the work and faith consultations
held to date, participants gave high praise to the "spiritual together-
ness" that they experienced:

> . . . the exhilarating experience of being with a talented yet diverse
> group of people who all really care about what we [the Church] are
> struggling with.

> The gathering and spreading of ideas, person to person, is invaluable in
> the development of any society. By bringing together so many facets of
> the Church, such consultations can only help the movement of the
> Spirit.

> . . . to feel part of a living community rich with differences, humor,
> suffering, love.

By providing opportunities for people to hear and tell each other's
story, consultations foster respect for the catholicity or diversity of the
Church and a deeper commitment to its one mission in the world.

It is suggested, therefore, that planners provide ample opportunity,
through reflection groups and plenary sessions, for the participants to

share stories about how they have related work and faith in their own lives. The evaluations of the national consultation indicated that the participants appreciated and would have enjoyed even more storytelling. It would appear that storytelling may even be more important than the talks designed to stimulate discussion. While the talks contextualize and focus the group's reflection, the storytelling yields the data that is, in the end, most useful to the church leadership.

The third principle is attention to the social and cultural context. In his summation at the national consultation, Fr. James Bacik said that perhaps Fr. John Coleman's lecture on "The World Today and Tomorrow: Its Meaning for the Church" should have come first. Several participants' evaluations echoed the same idea. Consideration of the social and cultural context in which we are Church provides a broad framework for the discussion about work and faith. To ignore that context is to be out of touch with both the trends that are capturing present imaginations and with the signs of the times through which the Spirit is speaking.

Planners of consultations, therefore, are advised to focus the discussion about work and faith by including in the program reflection on social and cultural questions like "What is happening in the world (the city, state, nation . . .) around us?" and "What kind of society do we live in?" Out of such reflection comes answers—or at least better questions—about what trends to encourage, what values to promote and protect, and what shape the ministry of the Church is to take.

Planners can promote reflection on the social and cultural context in several ways, including the following:

- invite participants to read John Coleman's talk before the consultation;
- ask someone to speak about the specific context of the parish or diocese in which the consultation is being held; or
- plan small group and plenary discussions on questions like those stated above.

The fourth principle is focus and purpose. One of the persistent challenges to consultation planners was the specification of focus and purpose. Many evaluations indicated that the presentations and reflection groups often strayed from the topic of work and faith, and that

participants and facilitators did not adequately follow-up on each other's comments, making the reflection more of a brainstorming than a
testing of ideas.

Perhaps, the novelty or the diversity of the topic necessitated such
brainstorming; perhaps, other reasons were the diversity among participants and the fact that they did not know each other well enough.
Brainstorming is effective, however, when it gives rise to a common
language and surfaces key problems and issues for discussion.

Experience with earlier consultations suggests that planners carefully
brief the presenters as well as the group facilitators so that the consultation will promote dialog focused on the topic and yield the information needed by church leadership. Particularly effective are presentations at both the beginning and the end of consultations that respec-
tively clarify the purpose and focus of the consultation and then summarize
its key insights. The repetition of a focus question in the course of the
consultation can keep the discussion on track. The question can be
phrased in any number of ways, including the following: "How effectively are you being ministered to?" or "How does the Church affect
your daily work life?" or "What kind of ministry will best empower
you, as a Christian, to be a transforming presence in the world?" Even
so, the inherent dynamics of a gathering of intelligent, articulate
leadership includes the unpredictable.

Furthermore, the emphasis being given to purpose and focus need
not obscure the value of the dialog between church leaders and laity.
The experience rated as most valuable by the participants in the
national consultation was the open dialog, regardless of occasional
lapses of focus and purpose. When effectively facilitated, however,
even these lapses can give greater substance and outcome to the dialog.

Program Planning Suggestions

Any number of agendas can be derived from the principles above;
we are only suggesting two possibilities here. Both stress the consultative process, and both are applicable to parishes as well as dioceses;
however, the second includes an educational process and may be more
appropriate for parishes.

Model A

The following agenda is divided into three parts.

1. Introductions. The aim of these initial activities is to introduce the participants to each other and to focus their attention upon the task of the consultation. Among the activities recommended are the following:

a) a clear statement of the basic question of the consultation (e.g., "What kind of ministry will best empower you, as Christians, to be a transforming presence in the world?";

b) an explanation of the bishop's or the pastor's reasons for requesting this consultation (e.g., the issuing of a pastoral statement on the topic of work and faith; the need to deal with certain timely local issues; pastoral planning for effective ministry to workers; the initiation of Christian professional groups);

c) a presentation summarizing the key variables in the specific social and cultural context of the parish or diocesan consultation; In preparation for the consultation, participants may be asked to read the Coleman talk and a summary of the key questions below.

2. Key questions. The three key questions of the consultation are derived from the basic question stated above. Each of these questions is introduced with an explanation and then discussed in smaller groups. The group reactions are reported to the larger assembly and discussed in a plenary session.

a) "When have I been ministered to?" This question probes the meaning given by the participants to the notion of "ministry."

b) "How is God present in my work?" In other words: "How is my work connected to my faith?" This question probes the participants' experience of the presence of God in the workplace.

c) "What kind of ministry will best empower us to be a transforming presence in the workplace?" Building on the other two questions, this question focuses on the shape that ministry should take. It will probably elicit some evaluation of present ministerial efforts, as well as some discussion around the commitment of the participants to bring their own gifts to the effort. The question, therefore, explores the ministerial needs as well as the ministerial gifts present in the parish or diocese.

3. Conclusions. Functioning much as Fr. James Bacik did with his final summation at the national consultation, one or perhaps more persons attempt to summarize for the whole group the general outcomes of the consultative process. This presentation answers the question, "What have we heard during this process?" Open discussion after the presentation corrects and/or expands upon the speaker's perception of the major answers to the basic question of the consultation. Participants are also invited to submit written reactions as well as an evaluation of the process. The data that may be most useful to church leadership subsequent to the consultation is the data that pertains to action suggestions; but other data (such as strong needs, major issues, and available ministerial gifts) may also be very constructive.

Model B

This agenda, like the first model, is also divided into three parts.

1. Listening. The participants listen to selected audio tapes or view the videocassette "Work and Faith in Society" from the national consultation and use the presentations published in this handbook for review and reflection.

2. Storytelling. Stimulated by the tapes, the participants then explore the questions as experienced in their own lives. The discussion focuses on the participants' stories and the issues they raise and *not* primarily on the concepts presented on the tapes.

3. Recommending. The participants offer their responses to the basic question of the consultative process: "What kind of ministry will best empower you, as a Christian, to be a transforming presence in the world?"

The Brockton Story

The national consultation was a three-day event; this afforded time for socializing, for continued conversation over coffee, for a banquet, as well as time for study, reflection, and dialog. It would certainly be possible for a diocese to host a similar two- or three-day event at a local retreat center or hotel. However, it is also possible to sponsor a one-day consultation, as did a region of the Archdiocese of Boston.

A regional coordinating group worked with Bishop Daniel Hart (who had attended the national consultation) to plan and conduct the "Brockton Regional Conference on Faith and Work." The following schedule for the one-day conference might provide some food for thought and give readers some ideas for planning their own such consultation.

Brockton Regional Conference

Faith and Work

October 27, 1984

11:00	Registration	
11:30	Assembly in Auditorium	
	Welcome and Prayer	Bishop Hart
	Goals of the Day	Jack and Sandy Logue
12:00	Lunch (Cafeteria)	
12:30	Introduction of Speaker	Barbara Killian
	"Is Christ in the Marketplace?"	Jack O'Donnell
1:00	Reflection Period	
1:15	Small-Group Session	
1:50	Return to Auditorium	
2:00	Introduction of Speakers	Sharon Moore
	"Keeping Faith in My Work-a-Day World"	Joe and Kathie O'Brien
2:30	Reflection Period	
2:45	Small-Group Sharing	
3:20	Large-Group Sharing (Auditorium)	
3:55	Follow-up	Brenda Natchek
	Closing Remarks	Bishop Hart
4:15	Sunday Liturgy	

During the course of the day, participants were asked to reflect on the following:

Religion is not just a part-time responsibility acted out in a temple or church on Saturday or Sunday. The specific role of the religiously committed lay person is not to serve the Church in the institutional sense, but to serve the world. We praise God not just in word and song at a liturgical service on weekends, but also in the work-a-day world in the five or six days between (Joseph Cardinal Bernardin).

Question: "What struggles do I have or will I have in trying to keep faith in my work-a-day world?"

Prayer (Adapted from the Christophers)

Father, grant that I may be a bearer of Christ Jesus,
    your Son.
Allow me to warm the often cold, impersonal scene of
    modern life with your burning love.
Strengthen me by your Holy Spirit to carry out my task of
    changing my part of the world for the better.
Despite my failures, help me to realize that my
    advantages are your blessings to be shared with others.

Make me more energetic in setting right what I find wrong
    instead of complaining about it.
Nourish in me a practical desire to build up rather than
    tear down, to reconcile instead of polarize, to risk
    rather than crave security.
Never let me forget that it is far better to light one candle
    than to curse the darkness, and to join my light, one day,
    with yours. Amen.

III.

SELECTED RESOURCES

The resources listed below are but a sampling of materials and organizations available for persons and groups interested in continuing study of the laity's life in the workplace. It is by no means exhaustive. Readers are urged to send their own suggestions for additional study to the Secretariat of the Bishops' Committee on the Laity. Please annotate all books and articles that you are recommending.

Audiovisuals

Laity: Work and Faith in Society. Videocassette, produced by Oblate Media Images. This 26-minute program highlights the major themes of the national consultation on "Work and Faith in Society." Moderated by Dolores Leckey, it brings together the diverse experiences of lay professionals in the workplace; a look into the theology and spirituality of the laity in today's Church. Order from: Sadlier, 11 Park Place, New York, NY 10007. $85.00.

Work and Faith in Society: Catholic Perspectives. Audio cassettes. Several of the major addresses from the national consultation are available on audio cassettes: "Professional Life: Vocation and Commitment," Dr. Sally Cunneen and Mr. Ralph Graham Neas; "The Catholic Spiritual Tradition," Dr. Doris Donnelly; "The World Today and Tomorrow: Its Meaning for the Church," Rev. John A. Coleman, SJ. Order from: United States Catholic Conference, Office of Publishing and Promotion Services, 1312 Massachusetts Avenue, N.W., Washington, DC 20005-4105.

Books and Publications

Called and Gifted: The American Catholic Laity. Reflections of the American bishops, commemorating the fifteenth anniversary of the issuance of the *Decree on the Apostolate of the Laity.* Washington, D.C.: USCC Office of Publishing and Promotion Services, 1980. Publication No. 727; $ .95.

Challenge to the Laity. Russell Barta, editor. Speeches delivered to the National Assembly of the Laity in 1979 at the University of Notre Dame. Huntington, Ind.: Our Sunday Visitor Press, 1980.

Decree on the Apostolate of the Laity (Apotolicam Actuositatem). Vatican II document. Washington, D.C.: USCC Office of Publishing and Promotion Services, 1965. Publication No. EC5; $1.75.

Laity Exchange Series. Four books, each addressing a different aspect of the laity's needs, concerns, and contributions: *Thank God It's Monday,* William Diehl; *Christians with Secular Power,* Mark Gibbs; *Laity Stirring the Church: Prophetic Questions,* Dolores Leckey; *Holy Worldliness,* Richard Mowr. Philadelphia: Fortress Press, 1982-1986.

On Human Work (Laborem Exercens). Third encyclical of Pope John Paul II. Washington, D.C.: USCC Office of Publishing and Promotion Services, 1981. Publication No. 825; $2.50.

On Human Work: A Resource Book for the Study of Pope John Paul II's Third Encyclical. Prepared by the Campaign for Human Development and the Office of Domestic Social Development. Washington, D.C.: USCC Office of Publishing and Promotion Services, 1982. Publication No. 847; $4.95.

The Supper Table. Maurice L. Monette. Retreat and adult education program based on the parables; challenges Christians to link the faith we profess with our daily lives. Table prayers, morning and evening prayers, and reflections on social responsibility are included to encourage the overflow of a justice-oriented spirituality into daily life. Available from Center for Concern, 3700 13th Street, N.E., Washington, DC 20017. $8.95.

Tracing the Spirit. James E. Hug, SJ, editor. A book of theological reflection on the experience of small communities engaged in the struggle for social justice. The reflections were sponsored and nurtured at the Woodstock Theological Center; many of the participants in the reflection groups were government employees. New York/Ramsey: Paulist Press, 1983.

Articles and Periodicals

Between Sundays. A journal dedicated to the issues of work and faith in American society. Edited and published by William H. Farley (a participant in the national consultation). Address: 16 Saw Mill Road, West Simsbury, CT 06092.

Gathering. A newsletter for small Christian communities. Edited by Robert Heyer of Sheed and Ward/National Catholic Reporter. Address: 115 East Armour, P.O. Box 281, Kansas City, MO 64141.

Gifts. A national quarterly journal for American Catholic laity. Produced by the NCCB Laity Secretariat and published by the USCC Office of Publishing and Promotion Services. $6.00 per year.

Initiatives. (In support of the laity's vocation in and to the world.) The regular publication of the National Center for the Laity, 14 East Chestnut Street, Chicago, IL 60611.

New Catholic World, "The Laity" (May/June 1984): vol. 227, no. 1359. Ramsey, N.J.: Paulist Press.

PACE. Series of articles written by Joe Holland: "Toward a Theology of Work: The Modern Degradation of Work"; "Toward a Theology of Work: Work as Co-Creation"; "Toward a Theology of Work: Some Pastoral Implications"; "Toward a Theology of Work: Toward a Holy Economy." Available from *PACE*, St. Mary's Press, Winona, MN 55987.

Organizations and Networks

American Catholic Lay Network. A network of lay-centered small Christian communities serviced by regional centers of lay formation. The lay network emphasizes a lay spirituality grounded in family and work, overflowing into a commitment and celebration of life as a seamless garment. Contact: Joe Holland, Center for Concern, 3700 13th Street, N.E., Washington, DC 20017.

Apostles in the Marketplace (AIM). Small groups of middle-class Christians who try to apply the Gospel to their professional lives. Contact: Eliane Raine, AIM, 320 Cathedral Street, Room 403, Baltimore, MD 21201.

Opus Dei. Approved by the Vatican as a secular institute in 1950, Opus Dei is an association of members dedicated to the apostolate of Christian witness and action and to the practice of an intense spiritual life without abandoning their own social environment or the exercise of their professions or secular occupations. Contact: Information Office, 330 Riverside Drive, New York, NY 10025.

The Servant Society. An association of lay men and women (ecumenical) dedicated to transforming the structures of society through their vocation to work. Contact: Howard Blake, Valle Verde, #D-502, 900 Calle de los Amigos, Santa Barbara, CA 93105.

ABOUT THE SPEAKERS

JOHN A. COLEMAN, SJ, associate professor of Religion and Society at the Jesuit School of Theology in Berkeley, holds a Ph.D. from the University of California at Berkeley. He is the author of *An American Strategic Theology* and several other books and articles. Fr. Coleman's current work is in the area of Christianity and citizenship.

DR. SALLY CUNNEEN, assistant professor of English at Rockland Community College, earned a Ph.D. in the philosophy of education from Columbia University. She is associate editor of *Cross Currents* and a lecturer for the New York Council for the Humanities. In addition, Dr. Cunneen is the author of *Sex, Female; Religion: Catholic* and *A Contemporary Meditation on the Everyday God.*

DR. DORIS DONNELLY, codirector of the Center for Spirituality at Saint Mary's College in Notre Dame, has been involved in higher education—teaching and writing in the field of theology—for over twenty years. Her special area of interest centers on discovering new ways and current role models to support what it is to be a contemplative-in-action.

RALPH GRAHAM NEAS, executive director of the Leadership Conference on Civil Rights, is a graduate of the University of Notre Dame and the University of Chicago Law School. He has worked as chief legislative counsel to two United States senators and has extensive campaign experience. Mr. Neas is founder and member of the Board of Directors of the Guillain-Barré Syndrome Foundation, as well as a member of the boards of Minority Legislative Education Program and "It's a Small World," a children's news network.

Cover Design:
Suzanne Novak
Denver, Colorado

Typeface:
Goudy Old Style

Typography:
Automated Graphic Systems
White Plains, Maryland